POP!

DESIGN CULTURE FASHION 1956–1976

GEOFFREY RAYNER
RICHARD CHAMBERLAIN
ANNAMARIE STAPLETON

British Library Cataloguing-in-Publication Data

A catalogue record for this book is available from the British Library

Designed and typeset by John and Orna Designs, London

Printed in China

Published in England by ACC Editions, an imprint of Antique Collectors' Club, Woodbridge, Suffolk

CONTENTS

INTRODUCTION

'MOD ENGLAND WAS GIDDY, BUT BENEATH THE DELIRIUM BUBBLED A CULTURAL REVOLUTION...' [1]

Between the optimism at the birth of Rock 'n' Roll and the disillusion of Punk, the Pop generation created a lifestyle which reached its apogee in 1966 in 'Swinging' London, and San Francisco's 'Summer of Love' in 1967. Throughout the 1960s Pop values and attitudes constantly challenged those of the wider society. From its dynamic genesis in the seminally important film of teenage alienation and rebellion, *Blackboard Jungle*, of 1955, which featured Bill Haley's iconic record 'Rock Around the Clock', to its negation in the anarchy of seventies Punk, Pop was probably the most significant cultural phenomenon in the second half of the twentieth century. Anglo-American in origin,

POP WAS DESTINED TO REMAIN ESSENTIALLY A MOVEMENT OF THE ENGLISH SPEAKING WORLD AND EVEN MORE SPECIFICALLY OF THE UNITED STATES AND BRITAIN ... BY DEFINITION, POP COULD ONLY FLOURISH IN A HIGHLY INDUSTRIALISED CAPITALIST SOCIETY ... [2]

Pop was a broad-based grass-roots culture whose exponents constantly blurred the boundaries of its primary vehicles of expression and communication – music, fashion and design – in a fluidity of artistic interests in the widest sense. These interests had their origins in a popular culture far too diverse and spontaneous to be identified with or controlled by a particular group of intellectuals or artists. This was particularly so in Britain where subtle connections between Pop musicians, Pop designers and Pop artists resulted from a shared common inheritance, many having begun their careers in the numerous art schools which mushroomed around the country following the Second World War.

The art school connection played a vital part in the success of British Pop culture, particularly design, Pop's primary form of visual expression. With the rise of consumerism, the mass-market and advertising in the post-war era, and the opening out of the educational franchise in the later 1940s to working class kids, an increasing emphasis was placed on the teaching of graphic design and illustration, often to the detriment – in the widely held view of the middle classes – of the fine arts. Fashion design also came to the fore as a popular area of study with both sexes. If not a Pop musician, photographer or fashion model, then being a graphic or fashion designer was considered by many young people to be the ultimate 'cool' career choice, and art schools became a fertile seedbed for a burgeoning Pop culture. Many leading figures in the Pop firmament moved from studying graphic design to Pop music or Pop art; the artist Peter Blake being an outstanding example, as are Pete Townshend of The Who and the members of the Rolling Stones, Charlie Watts and Keith Richards.

Amongst others, John Lennon, Eric Clapton, Roy Wood of the Move and Ray Davis of the Kinks initially studied art or graphic design, while Michael English, the leading British Pop graphic designer and muralist of the era, and his collaborator Nigel Waymouth, owner of the influential London Pop fashion boutique Granny Takes a Trip, set themselves up for a while as a psychedelic Pop band, Hapshash and the Coloured Coat, featuring the Human Host and the Heavy Metal Kids. Like English and Waymouth, the London-based cooperative of Dutch fashion designers The Fool – commissioned by the Beatles in 1967 to design clothing for their Apple store and the mural for its facade – also briefly transformed themselves into a band.

One of the most successful fusions of the various strands of Pop came in the early 1970s with the creation of the band Roxy Music. Bryan Ferry, the band's lead singer, had studied art at Newcastle University where he was taught by the Pop artist Richard Hamilton, and it was partly due to Hamilton's influence that the band was initially formed.

... THERE WAS A POWERFUL CONSTELLATION OF IDEAS IN HAMILTON'S ART AND TEACHING THAT WOULD LEAVE AN IMPRINT ON ASPECTS OF BRYAN FERRY'S CREATION OF ROXY MUSIC. [3]

The experimental artist, musician and record producer Brian Eno contributed an extreme, if somewhat other-worldly, flamboyant glamour and musicality to the 'Roxy' persona, which was also enhanced by clothing designed for members of the band by the fashion designer Antony Price, and the remarkable costumes for Brian Eno by the Pop artist and ceramicist Carol McNicoll. Out of this rich melange, Roxy Music itself became the ultimate Pop artefact. It was also an early manifestation of Pop's tendency in the 1970s to cannibalize its own origins, with the revival of interest in the fashions and style of early Rock 'n' Roll, particularly in Britain with the 'Teddy Boy' look, and 1940s and 50s American popular styling in general.

THE TEDDY BOYS WOULD FIND THEIR PLACE ON BRYAN FERRY'S FORMATIVE PALETTE OF INFLUENCES AND INSPIRATIONS – ABOVE ALL, IN THEIR DEDICATION TO A CERTAIN OUTRAGEOUS STYLE, THROUGH WHICH THEY BOTH DEFINED THEMSELVES AND MADE A FORCEFUL STATEMENT ABOUT THEIR SENSE OF IDENTITY AND PERSONAL ATTITUDE. [4]

At the cutting edge of this 1970s revival of early Rock 'n' Roll style and attitudes were the Pop entrepreneur and music promoter Malcolm McLaren; his partner the fashion designer Vivienne Westwood and the first incarnation of their shop in London's Kings Road, Let It Rock, which opened in 1971. Here they sold 'Teddy Boy' clothes, along with other 1950s influenced fashion and Rock 'n' Roll records and objects. In 1973 they renamed the shop, Too Fast To Live, Too Young To Die, and added ranges of Westwood-designed clothing to the stock derived from early 1960s 'Rockers' leathers and 'Bikers' gear. This was quickly followed in 1974 with yet a third incarnation, Sex, with the leathers transformed into bondage and fetish wear. In 1976, the shop reach its apogee as Seditionaries, the powerhouse of Punk, with, at its centre, the band, the Sex Pistols, the ultimate realisation of Westwood and McLaren's work of the previous five years.

In the 1960s, a similar creation of a Pop band, The Velvet Underground, had already taken place in the States, in a fusion of Pop art, music and design. The 'Velvets', considered by many the most influential and prophetic band of the decade, were the forerunners of many 70s proto-punk bands, such as the New York Dolls, the Ramones, and eventually, Punk itself. From 1965, the Pop artist Andy Warhol, formerly a leading graphic designer, managed and produced the 'Velvets', who toured that year in his multimedia road show, 'The Exploding Plastic Inevitable'. The band's first album, *The Velvet Underground and Nico*, was released in 1967, with a celebrated record sleeve, designed by Warhol, which bore on its front cover a peelable yellow banana covering a printed pink one. Throughout his career Warhol designed the packaging, or simply provided the illustrations, for record sleeves, such as his extraordinary sleeve for the Rolling Stones album of 1970, *Sticky Fingers*.[5] A leading member of the 'Velvets', the classically-trained Welsh musician and composer John Cale was married for a time to the fashion designer Betsey Johnson, who, when it opened in 1965, became principal designer for New York's leading Pop boutique, Paraphernalia. Here she frequently collaborated on fashion-linked events and 'happenings' with Warhol, and used the 'Stars' of his Silver Factory movies, Edie Sedgwick and 'Baby' Jane Holzer, as fashion models.

Although American popular post-war culture initially provided many of the ingredients for Pop design, in Britain since the 1920s there had been a growing interest amongst artists and designers in Victorian and Edwardian popular art, particularly nineteenth-century advertising. Following the Second World War an increasing number of books were published on the subject. This interest intensified in the early 1950s, when post-war popular culture, more particularly American, was almost forensically explored and analysed by the influential artists and intellectuals of the London based Independent Group, of which Richard Hamilton was a leading member. By the early 1960s – alongside young British Pop musicians reinterpreting and reinvigorating American Rock 'n' Roll and Rhythm and Blues music – many young British designers were synthesizing various aspects of British and American popular art and fashion, which they, as the musicians had with Pop music, then re-exported back to the States as Pop design.

Pop is now most often used as an adjective to describe both the dominant fine art movement of the 1960s and the various forms of expression created by Youth culture. However for Richard Hamilton, often called the 'Father of Pop', no such relation existed at the time between fine art and Pop. For him Pop art and Pop culture were one and the same – an art form complete in itself. In a radio interview with the cultural commentator and art critic John Tusa, Hamilton explained:

POP ART WAS WHAT WE CALLED MASS MEDIA, CINEMA AND TELEVISION; IT HAD NOTHING TO DO WITH FINE ART. WE CALLED IT POP ART, AND ELVIS PRESLEY WOULD BE A MANIFESTATION OF POP ART, AND ADVERTISING WOULD BE A MANIFESTATION OF POP ART, AND SO ALL THESE THINGS

WERE NOT SEEN TO BE SUSCEPTIBLE TO
TREATMENT. THESE IDEAS WERE NOT
SUSCEPTIBLE TO TREATMENT IN THE WORLD
OF FINE ART. [6]

During the interview Tusa expressed his personal opinion that:

HARD-CORE POP ART WAS ABSOLUTELY
ROOTED IN THE VALUES, THE SURFACES, THE
TREATMENTS OF THE COMMERCIAL WORLD.

In a letter in January 1957, Hamilton succinctly defined the characteristics of Pop as:

POPULAR (DESIGNED FOR
A MASS AUDIENCE)

TRANSIENT (SHORT-TERM SOLUTION)

EXPENDABLE (EASILY FORGOTTEN)

LOW COST

MASS PRODUCED

YOUNG (AIMED AT YOUTH)

WITTY

SEXY

GIMMICKY

GLAMOROUS

BIG BUSINESS [7]

Many designers who started their careers in commercial studios for advertising, packaging and illustration, made an easy transition to Pop, in which, unlike its antithesis, the Modernist movement, three-dimensional design had a minor part. Pop design (other than fashion) was essentially a two-dimensional graphic art form, closely related to commercial advertising, with which it shared silk screen printing as a primary method of production. Not only highly graphic in style, Pop was also extremely eclectic in its sources and willing to draw – often in unlikely and unexpected combinations – from any culture or period that fitted the particular needs of the moment.

POP ESCHEWED MODERNISM'S PURITY AND
WOULD BEG, STEAL OR BORROW FROM ANY
SOURCE THAT HAD VISUAL IMPACT AND

APPEAL. BY THE TIME A MODERNIST HAD RAISED AN OBJECTION ABOUT THE APPROPRIATENESS OF THE SOURCE, POP HAD LEFT IT BEHIND AND MOVED ON. [8]

The expressive and ephemeral nature of Pop design constantly subverted Modernist design concepts. Young designers in the mid-sixties, such as Paul Clark, then arguably Carnaby Street's designer-in-residence, indiscriminately silk-screened Pop decoration onto cheap mass- produced products: ubiquitous utilitarian white workmens' mugs; the plain inexpensive crockery used in 'greasy spoon' cafes, diners and factory canteens; disposable paper carrier bags and basic institutional tin waste paper bins. All aspects of design, from textiles and fashion, newspapers, magazines and posters of the underground press, and record sleeves, to the design of 'knock-down' plywood furniture, cheap tin trays, posters and other ephemera – all were deemed worthy of the Pop designer's attention. By elevating them to the status of fashionable objects of desire, Pop undermined generally accepted elitist ideas of 'good taste'. Paper, the quintessential Pop material, was used by the British designers Peter Murdoch and David Bartlett for the various disposable chairs and other furniture they designed in the mid-sixties, and by designers in the United States for that most iconic of Pop disposables, the paper dress. This fragile and ephemeral material received the ultimate accolade when it drew the attention of some of the most exalted in the Pop firmament, with Andy Warhol designing not only record sleeves, but also paper dresses, tote bags and posters, and Roy Lichtenstein, 'thro'away' paper plates and posters.

Banal and mundane materials and objects were favoured by many Pop designers, not only for their expressive Pop values, but also their low cost and low-tech qualities, essential for the 'do-it-yourself' manufacturing methods of what often amounted to a cottage industry, typified by fleeting ideas and rapid changes in direction. If Pop design was to remain 'up to the minute', low cost and easy to produce, then it's stylistic and often physical expendability required manufacturers to be small and flexible enough to respond quickly to new concepts, particularly in the dynamic world of fashion. In its first incarnation, in a former chemist shop in Abingdon Road, Kensington, the stock of the London fashion boutique Biba changed every Friday, when a completely new batch of clothing, designed by its owner Barbara Hulanicki, would arrive from the small 'rag trade' manufacturers she used in the east end of London. The new designs were eagerly anticipated by Biba's trendy young devotees, who filled the shop each Saturday and brought most of the stock, at easily affordable prices, to wear at whatever party, discotheque or concert they were going to that night. Writing of that time, the iconic 1960s fashion model Twiggy recalled that:

ANYTHING MODERN WAS WONDERFUL AND ANYTHING OLD WAS TERRIBLE. ... IN THE SIXTIES, ANYWAY, EVERYTHING HAD TO BE IN FASHION IMMEDIATELY AND THEN OUT AGAIN, CONSTANTLY CHANGING. [9]

The Pop lifestyle was essentially nomadic and many young people leading it lived in a frequently changing succession of bedsits, flat shares and, towards the end of the era, in communes and squats. For such a transitory way of life it was essential that Pop design was not only expressive, but also inexpensive and easily disposable; most Pop interiors were temporary triumphs of enthusiasm, improvisation and imagination. Living this way, other than hi-fi systems there was very little need for young people to invest in expensive consumer durables. Consequently the profits from Pop were, in the main, short term and, from the point of view of big business, small. Large manufacturing companies needed to invest in projects with a potential for reliably substantial returns over the medium to long term, but when Pop's rapid and unpredictable changes in fashion were added to the small short term profits of what was, in reality, a limited market, there was little incentive for big business to invest.

At the epicentre of Pop culture, the recording industry was exceptional in successfully combining the needs of big business with patronage for Pop designers. Some companies commissioned designs for record sleeves, packaging and promotional material such as posters, from not only leading graphic designers of the standing of Colin Fulcher (Barney Bubbles) and Hipgnosis, but also major Pop artists, amongst whom were Andy Warhol, Peter Blake and Richard Hamilton. However, despite the global impact and influence of their work, few Pop fashion designers, other than Mary Quant or John Stephen in Britain, and in the States, Betsey Johnson for Paraphernalia, were able to break successfully into the mass fashion market. Those involved at the cutting edge of Pop fashion, such as Tommy Roberts of Mr Freedom, rarely had more than one or two boutiques whose success was, more often than not, short-lived and largely dependent on the entrepreneurial and marketing skills of their individual owners. Despite her vision, even Barbara Hulanicki, in a mismatched and ill-fated partnership with the major British high street fashion retailer, Dorothy Perkins, was unsuccessful in translating her iconic boutique Biba up to the scale of the former Derry & Tom's department store on London's Kensington High Street.

As the era progressed — against the background of the economic and political problems of the late 1960s — many young people became increasingly anti-materialistic and anti-bourgeois, and there was a growing questioning and subsequent rejection, particularly in America, of the established order's promise of an bright technological future fuelled by the 'appliance of science'. This growing sentiment found expression in 1967 in the 'Summer of Love', which centred on the American west coast city of San Francisco — mother ship of the loosely structured 'Hippy' movement. The city rapidly began to rival London's position as Pop capital, and 'Mod' London's sharply-tailored dandyism was soon replaced with the romantic and flamboyantly eclectic style of Haight-Ashbury's 'Hippy' fashions. The style, predominately a Pre-Raphaelite faux medievalism, ingeniously mixed with the look of an Indian guru, a gypsy or peasant, supplemented with the buckskins, fringes, beads and feathers of the indigenous North American people and ponchos of Mexico, was so individual it was barely susceptible to successful exploitation by the commercial fashion industry. Joel Lobenthal writes that:

PREFABRICATED OFF-THE-PEG LOOKS WERE ANTITHETICAL TO THE ICONOCLASM OF THE ORIGINAL (HAIGHT-ASHBURY) COMMUNITY. [10]

Linda Gravenites, the renowned 'Hippy' dressmaker and close friend of the Rock star Janis Joplin commented:

WE GOT PRETTY SCATHING ABOUT 'STORE-BOUGHT HIP' THAT DIDN'T COME FROM THE SOUL. [11]

Basic unisex wear like flared cotton loon pants and jeans were widely available, and flowing locks were common to both sexes, but beyond this the realisation of the look was up to the individual. Describing early dances in the Haight-Ashbury community, Gravenites recalled:

PEOPLE DRESSED NO MORE BIZARRELY THAN THEY WOULD TO WALK DOWN HAIGHT STREET ... WE WERE DRESSING UP TO HAVE A GRAND TIME AND TO BE LOOKED AT, BUT MOSTLY TO PLEASE OURSELVES. THAT WAS WHAT WAS SO EXCITING. NO PURPOSE, NO ULTERIOR MOTIVE TO GETTING DRESSED EXCEPT FUN. IT'S PLEASURABLE TO LOOK STRANGE OR BEAUTIFUL OR MEDIEVAL OR AMERICAN INDIAN. [12]

Towards the end of the 1960s the tolerance and inclusiveness of Pop was ever more sharply focused and succinctly expressed, as various factions within the culture became increasingly radicalized and politicized. Many young people in Britain and America began to seriously question and reject the consumerist values, conformity, prejudices and intolerance of mainstream society and began to 'drop out', hoping to create an alternative society, the 'Counter-culture'. To the long smouldering injustice of racial inequality and the Peace movement's opposition to the Vietnam War, they added the issues of Gay Liberation and Women's Rights, and, between 1968 and 1970, their pent up anger and outrage frequently burst into violent protest.

Anarchy, radicalism, and 'agitprop' were words heard continually throughout 1968. In 1967 a peaceful revolution had seemed possible: by 1968 a violent revolution in Europe seemed not only possible but, for a few weeks, likely. [13]

From 1966 onwards, poster art and graphic design became in Britain and America, as it had in revolutionary Russia, the principal expression of the 1960s cultural and social revolution. The primary vehicles for protest were the pages and covers of the 'underground press', of which, in Britain, the most successful and widely read were the newspaper, the *International Times* (IT), and the satirical magazine, *London Oz*. A direct corollary of these was the remarkable series of 'underground' posters by the leading British Pop graphic designers, Michael English and Nigel Waymouth, who worked together as Hapshash and the Coloured Coat, and the series of 'Big O' posters, designed for *Oz* by Martin Sharp, the leading Australian Pop artist, designer and, with Richard Neville, co-founder of the magazine. The American satirical cartoonist and graphic designer Robert Crumb also made searing contributions to *Oz*, and, in the aftermath of the student uprising in Paris in 1968, to the French Underground magazine, *l'Actuel*.

A highpoint in Pop graphics is probably Heinz Edelmann's design of the Beatle's full length, gently subversive, animated film, *The Yellow Submarine*, whose graphic style was widely influential. Alan Aldridge, already a leading British graphic designer working in the 'Submarine' style was appointed art director of Penguin Books in 1965, at the age of 22. He left Penguin in 1968 to set up his own studio and that year was awarded, by John Lennon, the ironic title, 'Royal Master of Images to Their Majesties the Beatles'. He subsequently received many commissions from the band, one of the most important being *The Beatles Illustrated Lyrics* of 1969. He was also responsible for a number of swingeing satirical posters in the late 60s and early 1970s, amongst which was 'The Great American Disaster', commissioned by the London-based American burger joint of the same name.

In 1967, the leading mainstream American graphic designer Milton Glaser, joint founder with Seymour Chwast of the internationally-renowned New York based Push Pin Studio, designed the most Pop-inspired of his work, the superb poster of Bob Dylan, produced for inclusion in the packaging of the record, *Bob Dylan's Greatest Hits*. Another New York based designer, who, like Warhol, made little or no distinction between Pop art and design, was the Anglo-American Pop artist Peter Gee, who moved from London to New York City in 1962, where he met with considerable success. A close friend of the fashion designer Betsey Johnson, he subsequently exhibited with her friend Andy Warhol and the Pop artist Robert Indiana in the 'Word and Image' show, held at New York's Museum of Modern Art in 1968. He designed the logo for Johnson's Paraphernalia, America's premier Pop boutique, and packaging, which he silk-screened with images of Johnson and her friend, the model Penelope Tree. Throughout the era he created both remarkable Pop-styled commercial posters and packaging for a number of companies, such as the Chase Manhattan bank and Dupont, and more ambiguous silk-screened prints, which, intentionally defying definition, drift somewhere between fine art and design.

From about 1966, a new type of dynamic, graphic design, almost a contemporary urban form of folk art, evolved in San Francisco out of the West Coast Rock scene. Ostensibly, its purpose was to advertise the forthcoming appearance of rock bands at the various concert venues and dance halls around the city, but the posters themselves quickly became objects of desire and were eagerly collected in their own right. Mainly produced by the Rock impresario Bill Graham for his venue the Fillmore Auditorium, or by the Family Dog Collective at the Avalon Ballroom, the posters were largely the work of self-taught artists who, under the banner of 'Psychedelia', developed what is probably the most eclectic of Pop styles, a rich melange of nineteenth-century graphics and American advertising motifs, compounded with swirling Art Nouveau patterns and imagery drawn from comic books and sci-fi or gothic horror B-movies. Two of the five artists principally involved were Alton Kelley, a former motorcycle mechanic, and an ex-printer Wes Wilson. Two others, Stanley Mouse and Rick Griffin, had graduated, respectively, from backgrounds in the 'Hot Rod' circuit and West Coast surfing cultures, where they had already gained considerable reputations as cartoonists and decorators. The fifth, Victor Moscoso, the only one with a formal academic art training, had, after graduating from the Cooper Hewitt in New York, taken a masters degree at Yale, and in the late 1960s was teaching at the San Francisco Art Institute. His 'Neon Rose' series of posters for the small San Francisco rock venue, The Matrix, are considered both highpoints in the art of West Coast rock posters and of American Pop design in general.

The favoured vehicle of the American Underground press in the late 1960s were satirical pastiches of popular comic books, known as 'comix' to differentiate them from mainstream publications. The 'x' also emphasised their content, which focused on subjects dear to the

Counterculture: recreational drug use, politics, rock music and free love. Although 'comix' had been published since the early 1960s, it was not until 1968, in San Francisco, that Robert Crumb, the doyen of American underground satire, produced the first of his *Zap Comix* which, through his characters Mr Natural and Fritz the Cat, had a worldwide influence on the style and content of underground publications. In Britain, Crumb contributed satirical cartoons to *London Oz*, his poster, 'Honey Bunch Kaminski, Jailbait of the Month', being a major example. He was also a contributor to the British comix, *Nasty Tales,* and his work featured prominently in the trial of its publishers for obscenity in 1973. The evidence of one of the defendants, when speaking of the *raison d'etre* behind Crumb's satirical character 'Dirty Dog', is a succinct summation of the deeper motivation behind his work:

HE IS THE MOST OUTSTANDING, AND CERTAINLY THE MOST INTERESTING, ARTIST TO APPEAR FROM THE UNDERGROUND, AND THIS IS RABELAISIAN SATIRE OF A VERY HIGH ORDER. HE IS USING COARSENESS QUITE DELIBERATELY IN ORDER TO GET ACROSS A VIEW OF SOCIAL HYPOCRISY [14]

By 1970, the exotic medievalism and flowing robes of the 'Hippy' style were becoming passé and the wearing of denim by young people ubiquitous. Originally a form of tough work-wear, the popularity of blue jeans as a fashion item had been growing in the States since the late 1930s, a result of the rise of Western movies, fashions and 'Dude' ranch vacations. By the 1950s jeans were particularly popular with teenagers, who identified with the delinquent glamour and excitement of the jean-wearing anti-heroes portrayed by Marlon Brando and James Dean in Hollywood movies, or sex goddesses in jeans, like Marilyn Monroe in the Western, *River of No Return*. The canonization of jeans as objects of desire came in 1971, when Andy Warhol illustrated his sleeve for the Rolling Stones LP, *Sticky Fingers*, with a photographic image of the jean-clad lower torso of a well-endowed young man, complete with a real working zip. Printed denim was also immensely popular, probably the most spectacular example being that produced by Concord Fabrics, silkscreened with photographic images of the crowds at the Woodstock Festival in 1969, which was used both for jeans and a variety of other clothing.

Like so much else, the basic jean underwent a transformation in late 1960s San Francisco. Linda Gravenites recalled how she reinforced the frayed areas and rips in her favourite pair with floral embroidery, after seeing how a client, the Bay area folk singer Jean Ball, had embroidered tiny flowers along the hem of hers. Gravenites's decorated jeans went 'down a storm' in Haight-Ashbury and two years later they were on the market'. [15] By the early 1970s commercially embroidered denim clothing was worn extensively, but, like Gravenites, many also embroidered and painted their own. In 1975 a book devoted to decorated denim was published with the title, *American Denim, A New Folk Art*, a claim which the contents amply bears out. The concept for the book, essentially the catalogue of a 'denim art contest', [16] originated in San Francisco, and the entries, in their uninhibited, richly imaginative and exuberant individuality, closely mirrored the designs of West Coast Rock posters.

WHEN I DECORATED MY FIRST JACKET, I FELT THAT THE DESIRE TO COVER IT WITH EMBROIDERY AROSE FROM THE NEED TO SOMEHOW SET MYSELF APART AND ESTABLISH AN IDENTITY AMONG THE TEEMING MASSES OF BLUE-JEAN-CLAD STUDENTS. [17]

Commercially-produced machine-embroidered appliqués, known as 'patches', were also widely available at the time, in an apparently endless variety of designs, for applying to clothing to express where the wearer was then currently 'at', and very much an example, in Pop's determinedly non-literary culture, of 'the medium is the message.' Many amongst the young took Marshall McLuhan's aphorisms to heart, as one nineteen year old put it,

IT'S THE VISUAL AGE. READ YOUR MARSHALL MCLUHAN? THE MEDIA IS THE MESSAGE. MY CLOTHES ARE MY MESSAGE: THEY SAY THIS MAN'S THE GREATEST, THE MOST GEARED UP, THE MOST WITH IT. THEY SAY – BIRDS COME AND GET SCREWED BY THIS MAN ... [18]

An even more low cost form of non-literary Pop communication, expendable in every way, were printed tin badges. Between 1955-57, the Pop artist Peter Blake painted 'On the Balcony', an image of teenagers displaying their allegiances and interests through the cheap tin badges they sport, and the magazines and other popular ephemera which surrounds them. The art critic Robert Melville has described the painting as:

A METAPHOR FOR THE ACT OF 'COMING OUT INTO THE OPEN', OF ACKNOWLEDGING WHAT ONE STANDS FOR [19]

In 1961 Blake painted a 'Self Portrait with Badges', in which he portrays himself dressed in denim, with a variety of tin badges pinned to his jean jacket, the badges subtly creating a second portrait through the images and slogans they bare. In the photographer David Bailey's *Box of Pinups* of 1965, is a portrait of the photographer Michael Cooper, who, unlike Blake, wears his badges concealed inside his jean jacket, which he somewhat coyly holds open to allow them to be glimpsed. Cooper, whose portrait by Bailey is a knowing and witty inversion of Blake's self-portrait, was the photographer who subsequently worked with Blake on his iconic gatefold sleeve and packaging for the Beatles 1967 concept album, *Sgt. Pepper's Lonely Hearts Club Band*. By the early 1970s, tin badges were ubiquitous, loudly proclaiming their messages to the world in a visual cacophony of political, satirical and commercial slogans and images of Pop, Rock and film stars. A corollary of the badges was the sloganised T-shirt, which reached its apogee in the late 1960s. Having started life as a basic item of men's underwear, it became a form of outerwear for American blue-collar workers, frequently printed with a company's name and logo. By the 1950s, combined with jeans, it was an essential part of the teenage uniform, and at the end of the 1960s, like a kind of temporary tattoo, was instantly available, with 'on the spot' transfer-printed designs and messages, individually chosen from much the same, apparently, limitless selection of slogans and images as the patches and tin badges.

By the early 1970s most of youth's battles of the previous decade had been fought and largely won, and, with its vitality and energy dissipating, Pop culture began to fragment. There seemed little left to say or do and Pop design reached a crossroads. Having lost much of the anger and optimism that, paradoxically, had originally fuelled its rebellious questioning nature, the culture stagnated, continuing for most of the 70s increasingly directionless and self-satisfied. The ghost of Haight-Ashbury and 1967 had a long afterlife, surviving in the clichéd sequins, crushed velvets, brocades, silks, glitter makeup, ringlets and other florid excesses of the 'Glam-Rock' style. Many of the eras' Rock and Pop bands, like their music, fashions and attitudes, appeared at the time like bloated antediluvian dinosaurs to many, more radically-inclined young people. A flavour of some of these bands is captured, somewhat, in the satirical movie *Spinal Tap*, or in the work of graphic designers like Roger Dean, whose designs for the album sleeves of the Rock band Yes, or his 'Gemini' logo of 1972 for Richard Branson's Virgin Records label, typify the grandiose aspirations of many 1970s Rock musicians. Dean's graphic work subsequently made a considerable contribution to the visual style of a certain type of popular 1970s Sci-fi, the forerunner of many, now familiar, fantasy films, which, commencing with *Conan the Barbarian* in 1982, can still be seen in films such as the *Lord of the Rings* cycle or the animated 3D movie, *Avatar*.

Amongst the plethora of small art-based design studios and emporia that erupted around the turn of the decade were many short-lived fashion stores, which continued to follow familiar and well-trodden paths, such as Blueberry Hill, based in London's Kings Road, which survived all of six weeks in late 1970. However the best of these engaged the talents of a few highly original young designers who produced fresh ground-breaking work. Pop design's principal manifestation at that time is probably best described as 'Fun' design [20] whose chief exponent in London, was the Pop entrepreneur Tommy Roberts. Having successfully run Kleptomania, a shop in London's Carnaby Street, in 1969 Roberts opened the Pop boutique, Mr Freedom. Originally in the Kings Road, Chelsea, he moved the shop in 1970 to larger premises in Kensington Church Street, where he also opened a restaurant, Mr Feed'Em, in the shop's basement. The Mr Freedom style – largely the work of the talented young designers Jon and Jane Wealleans and Pamla Motown and Jim O'Connor – was pure Warholian Pop; it took inspiration from an eclectic range of sources, films and fashions of the 1940s, Disney cartoon characters, American baseball and football and, more significantly for the future direction of Pop design, 1950s popular culture and early Rock 'n' Roll. Another who referenced 1950s popular style in her designs was Miss Mouse, the fashion and textile designer Rae Spencer-Cullen, whose less well-known, but exceptional work in the 1970s helped to edge Pop ever nearer to the styles of the following decade. The origins of Post-Modernism were closely,

INTERWOVEN WITH POP ART DEVELOPMENTS AND A 1960S REACTION AGAINST THE IDEA OF GOOD FORM. [21]

Spencer-Cullen was part of an informal group of London-based artists, designers and stylists who between them created an important strand of sophisticated Baroque Pop, which, eventually, led directly to the New Romantics of the late 1970s, and subsequently became an integral thread in the fabric of British Post-Modernist design in the 1980s. Prominent in this group were the textile and fashion designer Zandra Rhodes and the artist and jeweller Andrew Logan, creator in 1972 of the 'Alternative Miss World' competition, an ironic event held annually for the remainder of the decade. Amongst others were the painter Duggie Fields, the journalist and stylist Chilita Secunda, the painter Lucianna Martinez de la Rosa, the hairdressers Leonard of Mayfair and Keith at Smile, the jeweller Mick Milligan, the Pop artist and ceramicist Carol McNicoll and the film director Derek Jarman. From the mid-1960s; more particularly, since New York's Stonewall riots in 1969, Gay Liberation became increasingly linked with the struggles of the counter-culture. By the early 1970s, it was politically and culturally, a 'hot' issue, and there was a strong element of almost defiant camp in the individual work of the members of the group, many of whom were gay and revelled in a joyously provocative use of kitsch. Carol McNicoll, then the partner of Brian Eno of Roxy Music, created extravagant exotic stage costumes for him, and a surreal ceramic dinner service for Zandra Rhodes, which mimicked fabric covered cushions, pillows and quilts, decorated with Rhodes' 'Button Flower' pattern.

Stylistically aligned with this influential group of avant-garde taste makers – identified by the cultural commentator, author and columnist, Peter York as 'Them' [21] – was the fashion designer Antony Price. He not only designed glamorous costumes for Bryan Ferry, then in the process of creating himself a Pop Art object, but also the costume – inspired by the poses and style of 40s and 50s 'Glamour Queens' and Hollywood 'Sex Goddesses' – worn by the model Kari-Ann on the cover of Roxy Music's debut album, which Price also styled. When considering criticism of the cover's apparent trivialising of women through frivolous and erotic fashions, he wrote:

FASHION IS NOTHING MORE OR LESS, THAN THE SERIOUSNESS OF FRIVOLITY. [22]

Price was also responsible for styling the eyebrow-raising and sexually ambiguous sleeve of Lou Reed's 1972 album, *Transformer*. The image of the raunchy young man on the back of the sleeve, wearing tight blue jeans, white T-shirt and a peaked leather biker's cap, the prototype uniform of rebellious 1950s youth, is another instance of Pop beginning to cannibalise its own history in the early 1970s. Only the T-shirt differs from the originals, being 'cap' sleeved, a Price innovation which became a standard detail of men's fashion in the 1980s. Price made a considerable contribution to the realization of Ferry and Roxy Music as the ultimate Pop creation, the summation of many of Richard Hamilton's ideas about Pop, of the process:

OF TURNING ONESELF AND ONE'S LIFESTYLE INTO A METICULOUSLY CONSIDERED AND POISED WORK OF ART. IT RAISED ISSUES OF GENDER, SEXUALITY, PERSONAE, IRONY, POP ART, POPULAR CULTURE, REVIVALISM, IDENTITY, FANDOM, HUMOUR, TECHNICAL CREATIVITY AND CULTURAL STATUS. [23]

Nick de Ville, art director of the early 'Roxy' albums, a former student and studio assistant of Hamilton, and a close friend and collaborator of Bryan Ferry, considered that:

ART HAD THE CAPACITY TO TAKE SHAPE WITHIN A VIRTUALLY LIMITLESS ARRAY OF MEDIA. [24]

As faith in the credibility of the established order began to crumble in the early 1970s, it was replaced amongst many angry and disillusioned young people by a mounting sense of alienation and aimless futility, which in turn led to a retreat from the disturbing realities of the time through an extraordinary return to Pop's origins of only some 10 to 15 years earlier. Although an attempt to escape into the mythic 'sunshine' world of the 1950s through a superficial idealizing of early Rock 'n' Roll culture, music and fashions, the revival lacked the energy, optimism and determination of the original. In Britain this was manifested by a growing, if somewhat shallow, interest in 1950s teenage fashions, such as the homogenised pastiches of 'Teddy Boy' outfits designed by the 'establishment' couturier Hardy Amies in 1971 for Hepworths, a high street retail chain of mens outfitters, or the more glamorised versions sold by chic London boutiques, such as Granny takes a Trip or Bus Stop. An interest reinforced by a steady spate of neo-Rock 'n' Roll music from teeny-bopper bands, like Showaddywaddy and Mud, or the early 1960s Rock 'n' Roller Shane Fenton, reincarnated as Alvin Stardust; all of whom regularly topped the British Pop charts throughout the decade. In January 1972, commenting on the origins of the revival, the journalist Ray Connolly wrote that:

THE FIFTIES ERA DID HAVE A QUAINT CHARM. IN A MUCH MORE REGIMENTED AND CONFORMIST SOCIETY THE NUMBER OF DAILY DECISIONS FACING EVERYONE WERE THAT MUCH FEWER, AND SOME OF THE MAJOR PROBLEMS OF TODAY WERE REMOTE AND WELL HIDDEN. IT'S A SELF-DECEPTION, OF COURSE, BUT LIFE DID SEEM CONSIDERABLY EASIER THEN [25]

The revival had, appropriately, first taken off in the States as early as 1969, with the spectacular performance at the Woodstock Festival that year, of the 1950s revivalist acappella group Sha na na, rigged out in the full glory of late 1950s New York teenage street regalia, 'pompadour' hair styles and greased quiffs. Another significant moment was the 1974 film, *Lords of Flatbush*, a saga of streetwise teenage New Yorkers, set in 1958, which featured performances by a young Sylvester Stallone and Henry Winkler. That same year, the TV sitcom, *Happy Days*, a cosy fiction of small town American teenage life at the end of the 50s, made its first appearance, and its 'greaser' hero, The Fonz, played by Henry Winkler, subsequently gained iconic status. The 1950s revivalist musical *Grease*, heavily influenced by the music and style of Sha na na, and Henry Winkler's Fonz character, was also a major hit of the decade, both on stage and film. An article on the phenomenon in *Life* magazine in June 1972 expressed the view that:

POP PSYCHOLOGISTS – AND MANY OF
THE KIDS – SEE THE FLIGHT TO THE '50S
AS A SEARCH FOR A HAPPIER TIME, BEFORE
DRUGS, VIETNAM AND ASSASSINATION. [26]

As the 1970s progressed, Pop culture, largely spent and exhausted, split in two. The proto Post-Modernist Baroque strand of Pop associated with the group of designers known as 'Them', although tinged with the underlying darkness of 1940s American Film Noir, was essentially 'Wildean' in its apparently frivolous 'Art for Art's Sake', non-judgemental, apolitical and amoral stance. It was instead, the advent of Punk that finally gave the *coup de grâce* to Pop culture. The reverse of the Pop coin, Punk became very dark indeed in its final incarnation in the mid 1970s under the Svengali-like influence of Malcolm McLaren and the menacing aura of the Punk fashions designed by Vivienne Westwood.

Punk's origins go back to early 1960s America and Garage Rock, a primitive style of amateur teenage Rock 'n' Roll music, which gained a certain amount of commercial success in the mid-1960s. The sound survived in the raw confrontational music of the proto Punk bands MC5 and the Stooges, which evolved amongst the increasing decay and violence of racially divided and crisis-torn late 1960s Detroit, centre of the American automotive industry, and original home of Berry Gordy's legendary Motown Sound. In the wake of a Garage Rock revival in America in the early 1970s, versions of what became known as Punk began to emerge, but nowhere more so than in New York, where the leading protagonists were the Ramones whose music spearheaded the advent of Punk Rock, and the 'Glam Punks', the New York Dolls. Shortly before their breakup in April 1975, the 'Dolls' were briefly managed by Malcolm McLaren, who had met them while in New York promoting his and Westwood's ranges of clothing from their London shop, then in its third incarnation as Sex.

On his return to London in May that year, McLaren, shrewdly sensing the nihilistic direction Pop culture was about to take, began to groom and promote a small unknown group, the Strand, whose career he had been, somewhat superficially, managing for some time. He rebranded them as a Punk band, the Sex Pistols, for whom he recruited a new lead singer, John Lydon – Johnny Rotten. Kitted out in Westwood-designed clothes from Sex, and supported with promotional material and album sleeves designed by McLaren's art school friend, the artist, graphic designer and anarchist Jamie Reid, Punk was suddenly up and running in a true Pop fusion of music, fashion, design, and, for McLaren and Westwood, big business.

Yet, despite what is often seen as its cynical and exploitative origins, Punk arrived at exactly the right moment to give voice and form to the growing despair of an increasingly dispossessed younger generation. Commenting on that time, John Lydon recalled that:

EARLY SEVENTIES BRITAIN WAS A VERY
DEPRESSING PLACE. IT WAS COMPLETELY
RUN DOWN, THERE WAS TRASH ON THE
STREETS, TOTAL UNEMPLOYMENT – JUST
ABOUT EVERYBODY WAS ON STRIKE.
EVERYBODY WAS BROUGHT UP WITH AN
EDUCATION SYSTEM THAT TOLD YOU POINT

BLANK THAT IF YOU CAME FROM THE
WRONG SIDE OF THE TRACKS... THEN YOU
HAD NO HOPE IN HELL AND NO CAREER
PROSPECTS AT ALL. [27]

The mood of the time was matched by Vivienne Westwood's designs for Sex, and, a little later, Seditionaries, the sinister obverse of the Fun revival of 1950s fashions, or the somewhat darker Hollywood glamour of 'Them'. Here in full-on confrontational mode were the jeans, leathers and T-shirts of the angst ridden rebellious 1950s anti-heroes – portrayed by Marlon Brando in the 1953 film *The Wild One* and, in 1955, by James Dean in *Rebel Without a Cause* – transformed into an ironic uniform for an army of angry, if often self-appointed, teenage no-hopers and dead-legs. The original teenage arrogance and virility associated with the jeans and leathers had transmuted into the mock servility and decadence of bondage clothing, and the once confident Union Jack motifs on the T-shirts of 'Swinging London' now exploded and disintegrated across the fronts of flimsy bondage shirts. Posters and record sleeves – other than fashion, the culture's primary vehicle of visual communication – bore a tirade of crude and overtly offensive anti-establishment images and language, carried out in a blitz of anarchic Dadaist-inspired graphic designs by Jamie Reid. For him, the medium was still very much the message:

YOU COULDN'T BE RESPECTABLE. WE DIDN'T
DO IT BY ACCIDENT, WE DID IT BY DESIGN.
WE WERE HORRIBLE BY DESIGN. [28]

For McLaren, Punk was neither the progenitor of New Wave music, nor a forerunner of 1980s attitudes and style, such as the New Romanticism of Westwood's 'Pirates' collection. For him it was, rather, the defiant end of an era:

THE CULMINATION OF SIXTIES PROTEST,
AN ART SCHOOL THING. PUNK WAS BASED
ON THE EXCITEMENT OF KNOWING YOU
COULD DO WHATEVER YOU WANTED.
THE SEVENTIES WERE JUST THE END OF THE
SIXTIES, AS THE NINETIES ARE THE TAIL-END
OF THE EIGHTIES... I DON'T BELIEVE PUNK
COULD HAVE LASTED MORE THAN A
MOMENT – IT WAS LIKE BLOWING THE
LAST FEW EMBERS OF THE FIRE. IT DIDN'T
PRODUCE MANY GREAT IDEAS, BUT A FEW
WERE GIVEN MIGHTY WORTH. [29]

Geoff Rayner
April 2012

NOTES

[1] Stern Jane and Michael, *Sixties People*, Alfred A. Knopf New York, 1990, p125.

[2] Livingstone Marco, *Pop Art: A Continuing History*, Thames & Hudson, London, 1990, p141.

[3] Bracewell Michael, *Re-make/Re-model*, Faber and Faber, London, 2007, p6.

[4] Ibid, p30.

[5] Marechal Paul, ed. *Andy Warhol – The Record Covers 1949-1987,* Catalogue Raisonne, Museum of Fine Arts, Montreal, Prestel USA, 2008.

[6] Hamilton Richard, interview with John Tusa, BBC Radio 3, 05.05.2002.

[7] Hamilton Richard, letter to the architects Peter and Alison Smithson, 16.01.1957, in *Collected Words*, Thames and Hudson, London, 1983.

[8] Whiteley Nigel, *Pop Design: Modernism to Mod*, The Design Council, London, 1987, p114.

[9] Twiggy, *Twiggy: An Autobiography*, paperback edition, Mayflower Books, London, 1976, p27.

[10] Lobensthal Joel, *Radical Rags: Fashions of The Sixties*, Abbeville Press, New York, 1990, p114.

[11] Gravenites Linda, quoted in Lobenthal, 1990, p114.

[12] Ibid.

[13] Whiteley, 1987. p182.

[14] *International Times*, Journal no 147, 09.02.1973. pp17-20.

[15] Gravenites quoted in Lobenthal, 1990. p112.

[16] Owens Richard M., Lane Tony, Beagle Peter, *American Denim: a New Folk Art*, Harry N. Abrams Inc, New York, 1975.

[17] Bernstein Pamela, 'Eureka, California', quoted in *American Denim*, 1975, p73.

[18] Whiteley,1987, pp157-58.

[19] Melville Robert, 'The Durable Expendables of Peter Blake', *Motif*, Journal no 10, Winter 1962-3, pp15-29.

[20] Whiteley, 1987. pp187-8.

[21] Collins Michael and Papadakis Andreas, *Post-Modern Design*, Academy Editions, 1989. p27.

[22] York Peter, *Style Wars*, Sidgwick & Jackson, London, 1980.

[23] Price Anthony, quoted in Bracewell, 2007. p385.

[24] Ibid. p384.

[25] de Ville Nick, quoted in Bracewell, 2007.

[26] Connolly Ray, 'The Fascinating Fifties', *The Evening Standard*, 04.03.1972.

[26] 'The Nifty Fifties', article, *Look* magazine, 16.06.1972.

[27] John Lydon, interview in *Punk Rock: an Oral History*, Robb John and Craske Oliver, Ebury Press, London, 2006. p97.

[28] McLaren Malcolm, article ' We were horrible by design', *The Independent*, 28.05.1991. p14.

[29] Ibid.

THE POP
IN POPULAR
1945–1956

POSTER, 'BLACK EYES AND LEMONADE'
DESIGNER BARBARA JONES
BRITISH, 1951

The artist Barbara Jones designed this poster for an exhibition of the popular arts she curated and organised with Tom Ingram at the Whitechapel Art Gallery in London's east end, as part of the 1951 Festival of Britain. The exhibition's title was adapted from a poem by the Irish poet Thomas Moore to read 'A Persian heaven is easily made, 'tis but Black eyes and Lemonade'. A pioneer in the field of popular culture, Jones later taught the Pop artist Peter Blake, who described her as 'A treasure trove of information about Popular Culture.'

POPULAR
ENGLISH ART
Noel Carrington and Clarke Hutton

PAT

LULU

TEXTILE, 'CIRCUS STRIPE', DESIGNED BY SUSAN WILLIAMS-ELLIS FOR BERNARD WARDLE LTD, BRITISH, EARLY 1950S.
INSET: BOOK COVER, *POPULAR ENGLISH ART*, WITH A DESIGN OF MERRY-GO-ROUND HORSES. NOEL CARRINGTON FOR KING PENGUIN BOOKS, 1945.
COVER DESIGN AND ILLUSTRATIONS BY CLARKE HUTTON

This textile and book epitomise the growing interest in popular culture in Britain during the 1930s, 1940s and 1950s, which eventually led to Pop.

25

ROCK 'N' ROLL
1956–1959

BOOK COVER FOR THE BRITISH PAPERBACK EDITION OF
THE BLACKBOARD JUNGLE, PANTHER BOOKS, LONDON,
1957. AUTHOR, EVAN HUNTER, AMERICAN, 1954

This story of teenage rebellion and delinquency in the American public school system was made into a ground breaking film in 1955, which is often credited with providing the launch pad for youth culture in the 1950s and 1960s.

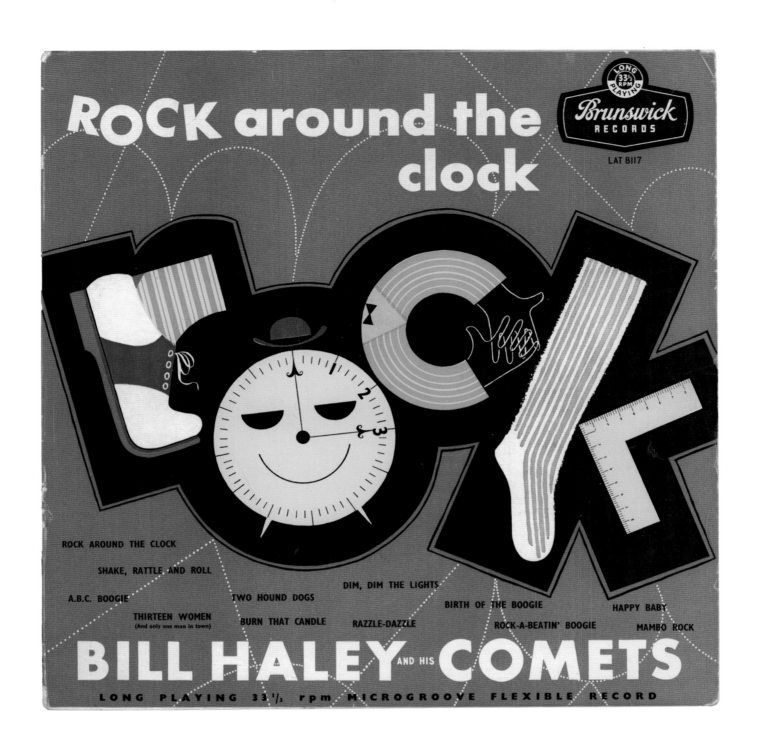

ROCK around the clock

Brunswick RECORDS

LONG 33⅓ RPM PLAYING

LAT 8117

ROCK AROUND THE CLOCK

SHAKE, RATTLE AND ROLL

A.B.C. BOOGIE

TWO HOUND DOGS

DIM, DIM THE LIGHTS

THIRTEEN WOMEN
(And only one man in town)

BURN THAT CANDLE

RAZZLE-DAZZLE

BIRTH OF THE BOOGIE

ROCK-A-BEATIN' BOOGIE

HAPPY BABY

MAMBO ROCK

BILL HALEY AND HIS COMETS

LONG PLAYING 33⅓ rpm MICROGROOVE FLEXIBLE RECORD

LP RECORD SLEEVE, *ROCK AROUND THE CLOCK*, BILL HALEY AND THE COMETS, AMERICAN, 1956

The film, and its soundtrack, which featured Bill Haley's iconic rock 'n' roll single, 'Rock Around the Clock', notoriously provoked scenes of wild and destructive behaviour from teen audiences, when first released.

ELVIS PRE

RICHARD

...SINGIN' MAN

...FIGHTIN' MA

...LOVIN' MA

FILM POSTER
LOVE ME TENDER
BRITISH, 1956

Elvis Presley, the King of Rock 'n' Roll, burst onto the world in 1956 with a string of extraordinary Rock 'n' Roll hits, amongst which were 'Heartbreak Hotel', 'Blue Suede Shoes' and 'Hound Dog'. Elvis's rapidly growing fame and status was further cemented that year with the world wide release of his first film, *Love Me Tender*. This poster for the film's British release is remarkable for successfully conveying, at that early date, both the energy and dynamism of Elvis's music and the power of his sexuality.

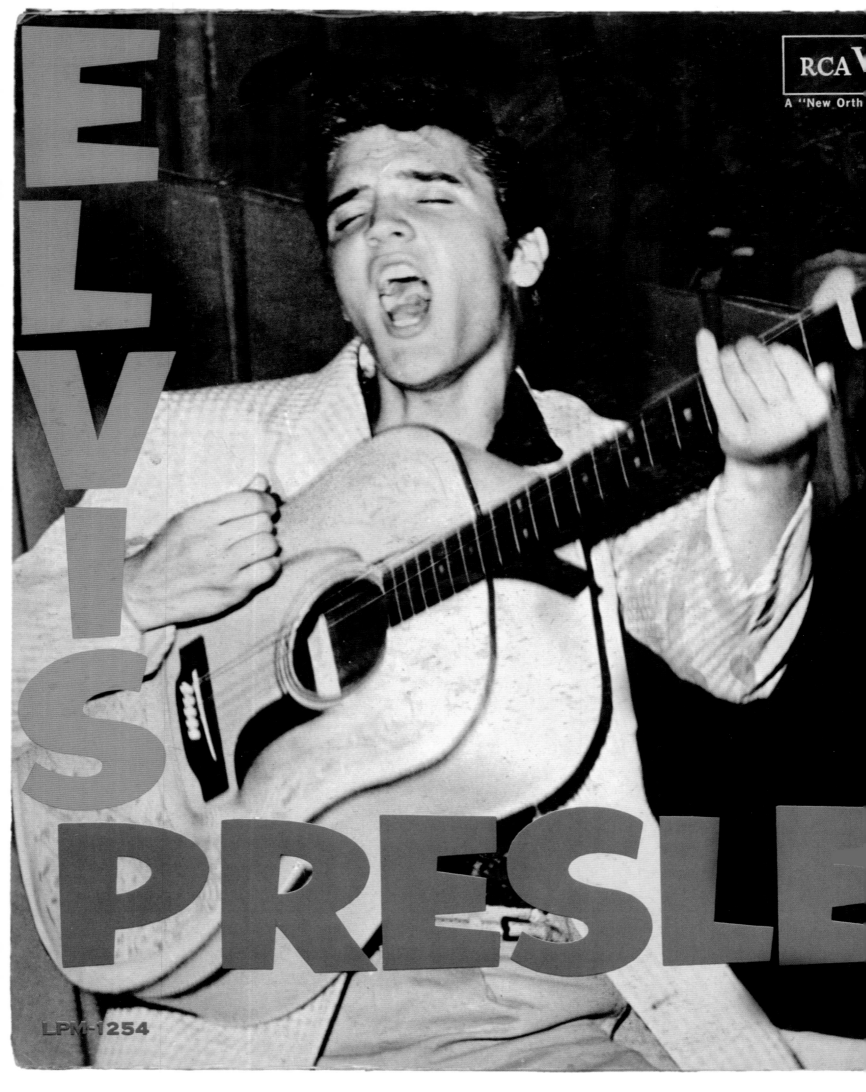

LP RECORD SLEEVE, ELVIS PRESLEY
AMERICAN, 1956

The 1956 sleeve of Elvis's first LP, its image equally as powerful as the preceding film poster, set a standard for Pop record sleeves, such as the homage version for the sleeve of the 1979 album *London Calling*, by the British Punk band, the Clash.

A COTTON 'BORDER PRINT' TEXTILE INTENDED FOR
SKIRTS FOR ELVIS FANS AND OTHER ROCK 'N' ROLLERS
AMERICAN, c1956

A SHORT FELT SKIRT INTENDED FOR ROCK 'N' ROLL DANCING, APPLIQUÉD WITH A DESIGN OF RECORDS AND MUSICAL NOTES, AMERICAN, c1957

'TEDDY BOY' DRAPE JACKET, BRITISH, LATE 1950S

The 'Teddy Boys' were the first 'teenage tribe' in post-war Britain. Mainly working class blue-collar youths, they were identifiable by their outfits derived from Edwardian dandy fashions and American Western styles, worn with heavily greased 'Pompadour' or 'Tony Curtis' inspired hair styles. From about 1954, they dominated headlines in the media for a few years with much-exaggerated stories of violence and delinquency, which culminated in 1955 and 1956 with the somewhat mythic trashing of cinemas during showings of the films, *The Blackboard Jungle* and *Rock Around the Clock*. The high point of their notoriety coincided with the Rock 'n' Roll era between 1956 and 1959.

'MARTINI LABEL' PRINTED COTTON SKIRT
BRITISH, c1956

This textile is a particularly early example of Pop's use of commercial advertising for decorative purposes. Whilst a successful marketing tool for Martini, it also expressed the sophisticated taste of the wearer for glamorous and sexy Italian drinks, and by association, exciting foreign travel. It was particularly popular between 1956 and 1957 with Rock 'n' Roll fans for full circle skirts worn with layer upon layer of stiffened petticoats.

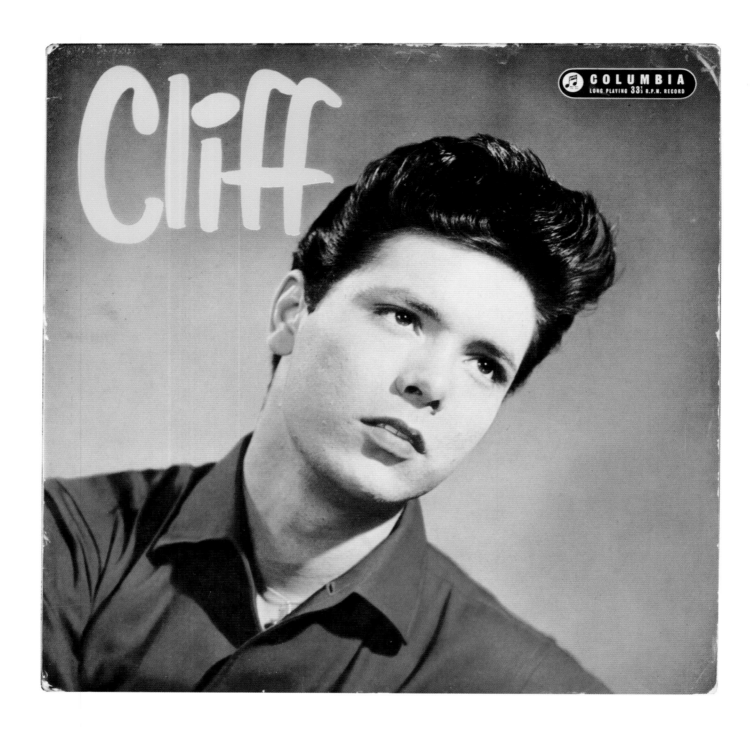

THE SLEEVE OF CLIFF RICHARD'S FIRST LP RECORD
BRITISH, 1959

Although there had been slightly earlier British Pop stars such as Tommy Steele, it was not until the release of 'Move It', the debut single of Cliff and his group the Drifters, in late August 1958, that Britain had a Rock 'n' Roll star to equal the Americans. Cliff's early recordings with his band the Drifters, later renamed the Shadows, were pure exciting Rock 'n' Roll, although he soon succumbed to the allure of mainstream show biz. This cover is one of the first in a long succession of glamorised 'boy next door' images of Pop stars aimed by the recording industry at the female teenage market.

'TEDDY BOYS', FILM POSTER FOR THE FRANCO-BELGIAN RELEASE OF THE BRITISH FILM, SERIOUS CHARGE, 1959

Like most British and American Pop stars of the late 1950s and early 1960s, Cliff Richard was quickly found a role in a film suitable for marketing him as a teen idol. The storyline of Serious Charge – teenage delinquency, violence and sexuality, redeemed through the efforts of a clergyman – was intended to exploit the teen market, while reassuring adult society. However, the design of this poster, in the garish style of the covers of cheap throwaway pulp fiction novels, sensationalises the film's content of delinquency and sexuality at the expense of its redemptive theme.

MAN'S SLICKER JACKET
PRINTED COTTON
BRITISH, c1957

The early use of photographic images of film stars for the design of the textile used for this slicker jacket is remarkably prescient of Pop textiles in the later 1960s and early 1970s, many of which were inspired by late 1950s textiles such as this.

TEXTILE, PRINTED WITH THE NAMES OF POP STARS
BRITISH, c1957

A cotton textile printed with the names of Pop stars, intended for the skirts of Rock 'n' Roll fans.

LEFT: COFFEE TABLE IN THE FORM OF A PIANO. BRITISH, c1958. OPPOSITE: RECORD CABINET, BRITISH, c1958

Produced in very inexpensive and extremely lightweight materials, these insubstantial pieces of furniture epitomise the ephemeral, transitory and often surreal nature of much Pop design. Gimmicky, witty, low cost and aimed at youth, they are a summation of Richard Hamilton's classic definition of Pop.

TREBLE CLEF PLANT STAND, BRITISH, c1958

Like the preceding piano shaped coffee table and record cabinet, this inexpensively- produced surreal plant stand is a summation of Hamilton's definition of Pop, and like them, refers in its design to Rock 'n' Roll music.

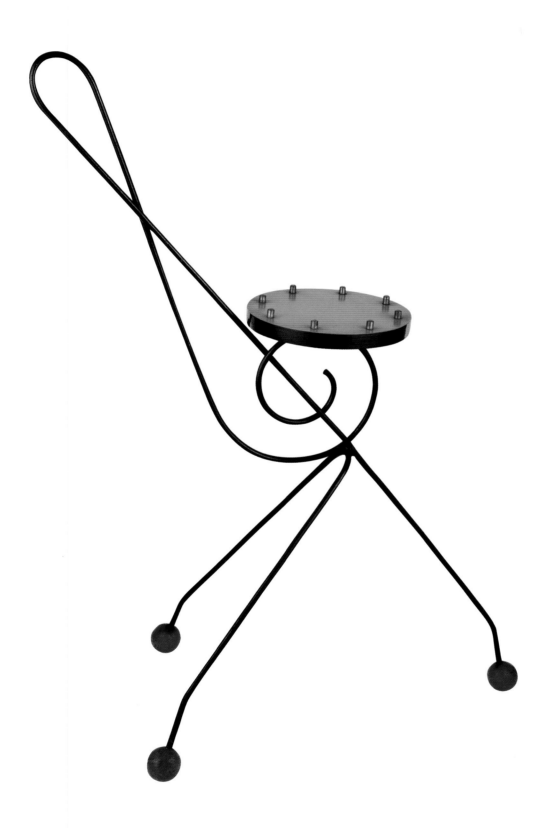

A COTTON TEXTILE PRINTED WITH A HIGHLY
EXPRESSIVE DESIGN OF THE IDEALISED TEENAGE
LIFESTYLE, BRITISH, c1957

LP RECORD SLEEVE, GENE VINCENT, AMERICAN, 1956

Like Elvis Presley, Gene Vincent suddenly burst on the world in 1956. The image on this sleeve of his second LP, *Gene Vincent and the Blue Caps*, portrays the group as a vaguely-defined street tribe of slightly menacing teenage delinquents. From the end of the 1950s, Vincent's revamped leather-clad persona successfully chimed with that of the 'Rockers' and 'Greasers' of the biker community.

ROCKER'S GEAR: JACKET, HELMET, BELT AND GOGGLES BRITISH EARLY 1960S. COVER OF PAPERBACK BOOK *MOTORBIKE* BY BERNARD KOPS, BRITISH FOUR SQUARE BOOKS, 1962

Although a proto-teen tribe culturally related in Britain to the Teddy Boys, unlike them, the 'Rockers', or 'Ton Up Boys', survived the Rock 'n' Roll era, to thrive throughout the 1960s and well beyond. They first emerged as an identifiable group around the same time as the 'Teds'. The defining moment being the release in America, on 30th December 1953, of *The Wild One*, probably the first post-war movie of teenage alienation and rebellion. Although an almost instant critical success in America, the movie was banned in Britain until 1968. However, countless iconic photographic images of its star Marlon Brando as the glamorously-delinquent biker leader Johnny Strabler, set the style for bikers in America and Britain in the 1950s and 1960s. (Rocker's gear courtesy of Simon and Mel Andrews)

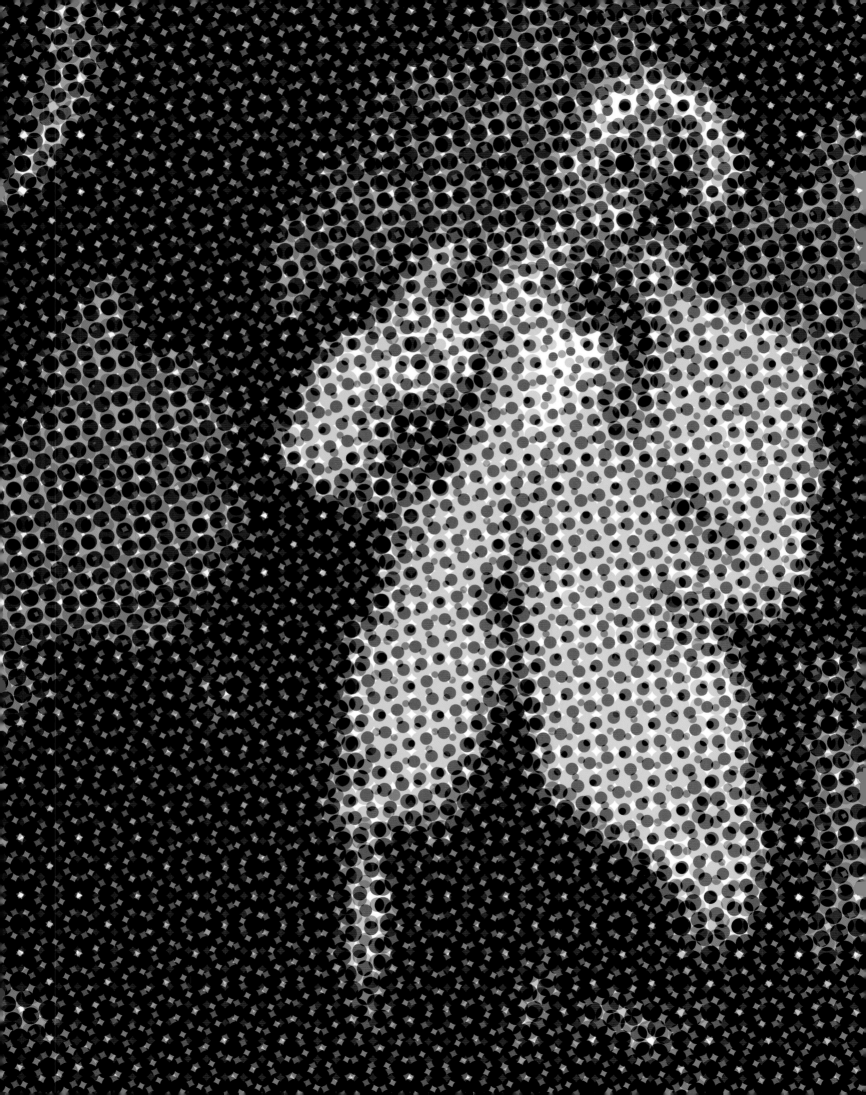

'MAD MEN':
MODERNISTS
INTO MODS
1960–1963

TAKE FIVE
THE DAVE BRUBECK QUARTET

EP RECORD, *TAKE FIVE,* THE DAVE BRUBECK QUARTET, 1961

Following the demise of Rock 'n' Roll in the late 1950s, Pop music was largely reduced to a fleeting and inconsequential form of teenage entertainment. It was Modern Jazz musicians like Miles Davis, Thelonious Monk and Ray Charles, and singers like Ella Fitzgerald and Dinah Washington who provided the definitive soundtrack of the early 1960s. Although there was a brief vogue for 'Trad' Jazz, until the arrival of the Beatles in late 1962 and Rhythm and Blues music the following year, for most 'switched-on' youth, Modern Jazz was where it 'was at'. Its 'cool' sounds perfectly complimenting the elegant simplicity of early Mary Quant-inspired 'Mod' fashions and the sharp Italian styling of young mens' 'Modernist' suits and accessories. At the crest of the Modern Jazz wave in 1961 *Take Five* became a unexpected hit for the Dave Brubeck Quartet on both sides of the Atlantic.

TEA TOWEL, SCREEN PRINTED COTTON, LAURA AND BERNARD ASHLEY, BRITISH, c1958

The Ashleys began what subsequently became their major international company by silk-screening tea towels on the kitchen table of their Chelsea home in London in the mid-1950s. These early products were designed in a high Pop style that utilised amusing nineteenth and early twentieth-century advertisements that later became a mainstay of Pop graphic design.

52 MODERNISTS INTO MODS 1960–1963

WHAT WILL YOU DO

IN THE

LONG, COLD, DARK, SHIVERY EVENINGS,

WHEN YOUR HEALTH AND CONVENIENCE COMPEL YOU TO STAY

INDOORS ?

WHY!!! HAVE A PHONOGRAPH, OF COURSE.

It is the FINEST ENTERTAINER in the WORLD.

There is nothing equal to it in the whole Realm of Art.

It imitates any and every Musical Instrument, any and every natural sound, faithfully:

the **HUMAN VOICE**, the **NOISE OF THE CATARACT**, the **BOOM OF THE GUN**, the **VOICES OF BIRDS OR ANIMALS**.

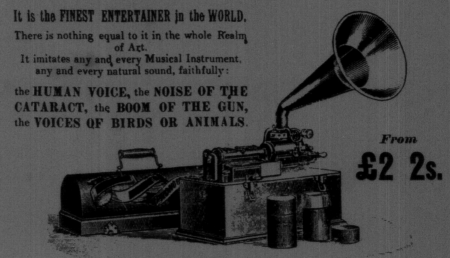

From

£2 2s.

THE GREATEST MIMIC.

A Valuable Teacher of Acoustics. Most Interesting to Old or Young. A Pleasure and Charm to the Suffering, bringing to them the Brightness and Amusements of the outside World by its faithful reproductions of Operas, New Songs, Speeches, &c.

EVERY HOME WILL sooner or later have its PHONOGRAPH as a NECESSITY.

HAVE YOURS NOW; you will enjoy it longer.

famous French actor, writes:

TRANSLATION OF THE LETTER

" Your wonderful Gramophone has at last given me what I have so much desired ; the surprise and (shall I confess it ?) the pleasure of hearing myself ! I have heard the recitation ' Des Limacons, which I recite in the rôle of M. de la Motte, in the ' Mercure Galant ' of Boursault, and my word . . . . I did what I have seen the public do for a long time, I laughed. Thank you for having made me amuse myself—that does not often happen to me—and I congratulate you on your Gramophone, which must render great services to everybody.

GENTLEMEN,—

" I have much pleasure in stating that I have heard your Monarch Gramophone, and that I consider it a very remarkable instrument of its kind, and quite the most perfect that I have ever heard. It reproduces the human voice to such a fine point, that in listening to the records of Caruso, Plançon, &c., it seemed to me as if those artists were actually singing in my saloons. I have never heard anything to equal it.

POSTER FOR LLOYD'S BOOKSHOP, WIMBLEDON, LONDON. PETER GEE ANGLO-AMERICAN, 1961

Like the Laura Ashley tea towel, this poster by Peter Gee is an early example of high Pop graphic design. It makes clever reference to the bookshop it was designed for by utilising a wide variety of printer's fonts and symbols printed on cheap brown wrapping paper. Shortly after designing this poster Gee left London for New York where he pursued an extremely successful career as a Pop artist, designer and teacher.

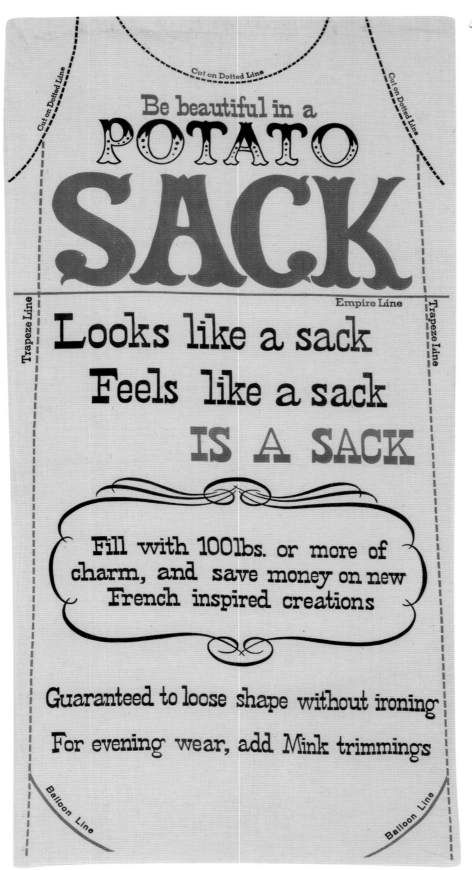

'POTATO SACK'
CHARTERHOUSE
MANUFACTURING
CO., NEW YORK
AMERICAN, c1960

This potato sack, screen-printed in Pop-style playbill lettering, is a witty and ironic Pop satire on the radical new French fashions, mainly designed by Pierre Cardin, that were launched in the late 1950s. It particularly satirises Cardin's 'Sac' dress, potato sacks having long been used as dresses by America's rural poor, particularly in the Great Depression of the 1930s. It was with reference to this tradition that Marilyn Monroe posed for publicity photos in the mid-1950s, wearing only high heels and a belted sack, with the headline, 'She looks beautiful, even in a potato sack'.

SAC DRESS WITH A DETACHABLE HALF BELT, DESIGNED BY MARY QUANT, BRITISH, c1959-60 STILETTO HEEL SHOES, DESIGNED AND MADE IN ITALY FOR THE BRITISH SHOE RETAILER, VERNON HUMPAGE, c1960

Quant's early fashion designs, and her Chelsea boutique, Bazaar, initiated a revolution in young women's fashions and fashion retailing in Britain and eventually, the world. Her work later inspired the 'Mod' fashions of 'Swinging' London, and her influence quickly spread to America, when she designed her first mass-produced ranges for the J. C. Penny chain of stores in 1962. Versions of Quant's early designs were worn by 'cool Modernist chicks' in music venues, like Ronnie Scott's club, the Marquee or the Flamingo, which sprung up in London and major provincial cities in the late 1950s and early 60s. These early 'Mod' outfits were invariably worn with extremely elegant stiletto shoes, preferably Italian or, at least, Italian styled.

OPPOSITE: YOUNG MAN'S 'MODERNIST' SUIT, BRITISH c1962. BELOW: 'GO-GETTER'S', POINTED SHOES, MADE IN ITALY AND STYLED BY ALBERTO OF MILAN, c1961 RIGHT: TWO 'SLIM JIM' POP-INFLUENCED TIES BY 'ROOSTER', AMERICAN, EARLY 1960S

At the beginning of the decade, sophisticated young 'Modernists' – originally Modern Jazz devotees – made a major contribution to the sartorial revolution in mens fashions in the 1960s. Rather than being 'dedicated followers of fashion', they were instead, style-obsessed lower middle class and working class dandies, who competitively initiated and evolved changes in fashion amongst themselves. Their sharp style was heavily influenced by Italian fashion or the radical male fashion designs of Pierre Cardin, whose styling could be seen in clothes available in pioneering male boutiques like Vince or John Stephen's His Clothes. Although by 1963 'Modernists' had evolved into 'Mods', they were far from being members of the teenage scooter tribe, younger brothers of the 'Teds', now usually associated with the sobriquet 'Mod'. They were, rather, the forerunners of the fashionable 'exquisites' of 'Swinging London'. Prominent amongst these proto 'Mods', already well known on the London club scene in the early 1960s, were Long John Baldry, then lead singer of the Rhythm and Blues band, the Cyril Davis R&B Allstars, Rod Stewart, (aka 'Rod the Mod') and Marc Bolan, a leading 'Mod' or 'Face' of 1962.

MAN'S COTTON TOP BY VINCE, BRITISH, c1960 OPPOSITE: ADVERTISEMENT FOR VINCE, WITH SEAN CONNERY MODELLING THIS TOP, c1960. BROCHURE FOR VINCE, SPRING 1962

Vince, the first fashion boutique for men in Britain, was opened in 1954 by Bill Green in the Soho area of central London. The impact of Vince on men's fashion in the 1960s cannot be overestimated. Originally catering to an almost exclusively gay clientele, Vince soon became an 'In' destination for many of London's Bohemian male fringe, amongst who were Peter Sellers and Sean Connery, and visiting travellers such as Picasso, even the King of Denmark. Green imported fashions from France and Italy which he augmented with his own designs, adopting materials for men's clothes probably not used since the Regency, such as velvet and silk, and even mattress ticking for trousers. He also imported Levi jeans from the States, then a rarity, and French-styled clothes in pale blue, even pink, faded denim. Although expensive and exclusive, the Vince style had a far reaching influence on mens 'Mod' fashion through its many imitators. None more so than a former Vince sales assistant, John Stephen, who began the transformation of Carnaby Street as the fashion Mecca of 'Swinging' London when he opened his first 'Vince' style menswear boutique there, His Clothes, in 1957. (Vince brochure courtesy of Philippe Garner Collection)

VINCE
VINCE GREEN

mans shop 1962

contemporary design in leisure wear

Vince

CAPRI SHIRT
No. 622 Typical of our exclusive styling in Navy/White striped DENIM. Cut on generous lines and tapering to waist.

Please state chest size. Add 1/- post and packing. **47/6**

Vince

EXCLUSIVE JEANS
No. 306 French style in "Faded" Blue DENIM with 2 front and 2 hip pockets **38/6**

No. 307 Tailored in DRILL with 2 front and 2 hip pockets. IN BLACK OR THE NEW RIVIERA COLOUR, SKY BLUE. **42/-**

Please state waist and inside leg measurements. All Jeans taper to 16in. Add 1s. 8d. post and packing.
24-page illustrated catalogue will be sent on request.

vince man's shop

15 Newburgh Street, Foubert's Place, Regent Street, London, W.1. GER 3730
Open Mon. Tues. Wed. Fri. 9 to 5.30 p.m. Thurs. 9 to 7 p.m. Sat. 9 to 3 p.m.

Vince Leisure Wear also on sale at James Grose Ltd. 379 Euston Road, N.W.1, and at Marshall & Snelgrove at Leeds, Manchester and Leicester

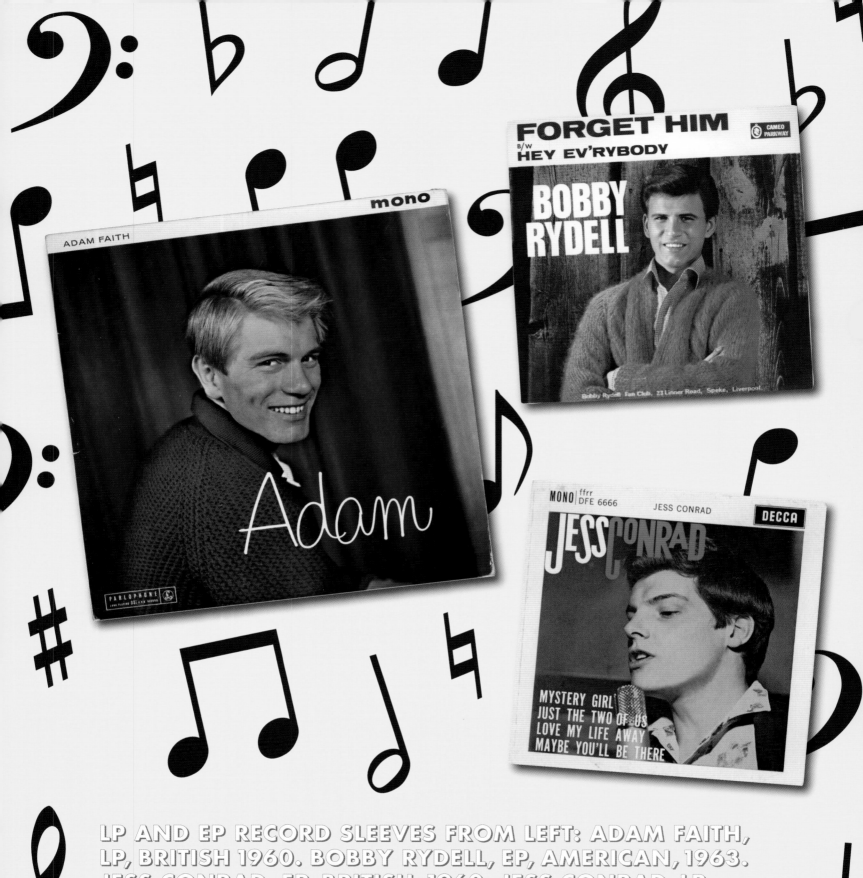

LP AND EP RECORD SLEEVES FROM LEFT: ADAM FAITH, LP, BRITISH 1960. BOBBY RYDELL, EP, AMERICAN, 1963. JESS CONRAD, EP, BRITISH, 1960. JESS CONRAD, LP, BRITISH, 1961. JOHN LEYTON, LP, BRITISH, 1961

By 1960 Rock 'n Roll was exhausted and, until the advent of the Beatles in 1962, Pop music largely existed in a 'no man's land', epitomised by the 'boy next door' singer, blatantly styled and promoted by record companies to exploit the female teen market. Probably the best of these recordings is the work of the brilliant but eccentric independent British record producer, Joe Meek, and his stable of 'boy' singers, amongst whom were John Leyton and Jess Conrad.

62 MODERNISTS INTO MODS 1960–1963

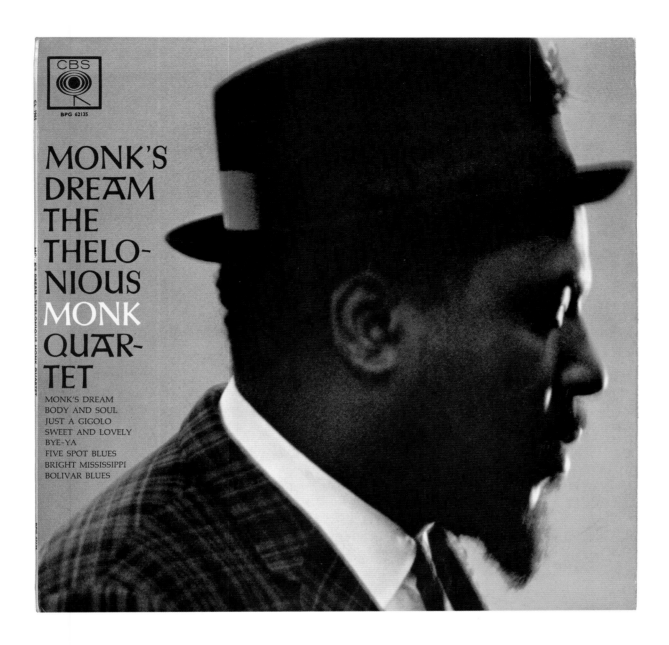

LP RECORD, *MONK'S DREAM*, THE THELONIOUS MONK QUARTET AMERICAN, 1963

The Modern Jazz of Thelonious Monk was one of the 'coolest' sounds of the early 1960s, and Monk's image on this sleeve, with his sharp 'pork-pie' hat and jazz beard, is a succinct summation of 'cool' Modernist style.

FURNISHING TEXTILE, 'MODERN JAZZ MUSICIANS', A. SANDERSON & SON LTD BRITISH, c1961

This textile is a classic example of the elegant sophistication that Pop design achieved in the early 1960s.

64 MODERNISTS INTO MODS 1960–1963

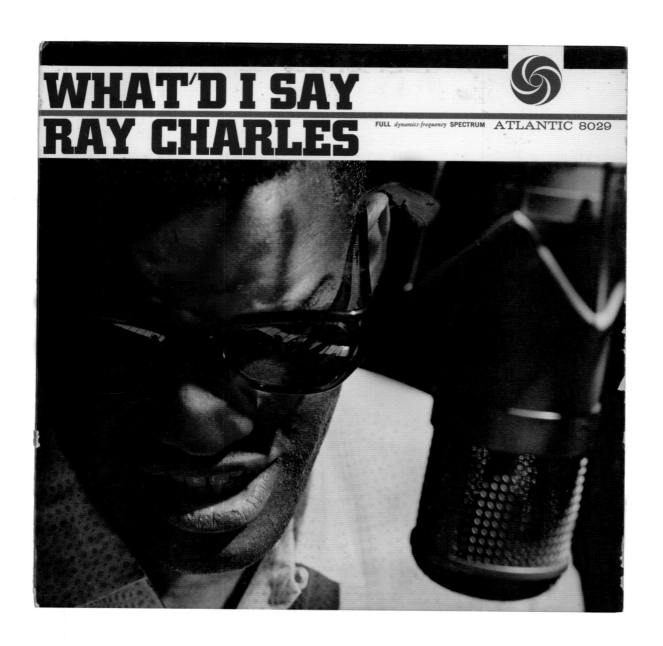

SLEEVE OF LP RECORD, WHAT'D I SAY
RAY CHARLES, AMERICAN, 1959

Ray Charles's song, 'What'd I Say', although recorded in 1959, was an important part of the general soundtrack of the early 1960s, and a powerful crossover number which bridged jazz and what became known a little later as Soul music. Its sleeve, a stark photographic image of Charles performing, is reminiscent in its expressive intensity of the sleeve of Elvis Presley's first album.

WALLPAPER, JAZZ ALBUMS AND MUSICIANS
BRITISH, c1962

The design of this sophisticated Pop wallpaper refers directly to the sleeve of Ray Charles's 1959 LP, *The Genius of Ray Charles*, and the sleeves of other Modern Jazz albums popular at the time, such as the Modern Jazz Quartet's, *Third Stream Music*, 1960, and the LP, *Thelonious Monk with John Coltrane*, 1961. There is also an image of the singer Ella Fitzgerald, and visual references to Acker Bilk and 'Trad' Jazz, and Lonnie Donagan's 1956 EP, *Skiffle Session*.

66 MODERNISTS INTO MODS 1960–1963

MAN'S BLACK VINYL TOP BY MELDA CONTINENTAL LEISURE WEAR, BRITISH, c1963

The first British 'Swinging '60s' television series, The Avengers, launched in 1961, provided the template for the many 'offbeat' detective and spy series so popular internationally throughout the decade. Honor Blackman, the female star of the second series, notoriously played the lead role of Dr Cathy Gale, a black leather and vinyl-clad, sexy, witty and liberated dominatrix and judo expert. Dedicated to the defeat of evil, with implied links to British intelligence, in many ways Cathy Gale was the female counterpart of Sean Connery's contemporary film character, James Bond. Indeed, Honor Blackman subsequently played opposite Connery as Bond girl Pussy Galore in the 1964 movie, *Goldfinger*. Between 1962 and 1964, the influence of Cathy Gale's clothes, designed by Fredericke Starke, some of which were made up by John Sutcliffe, publisher of the *AtomAge* fetish magazine, sparked a brief 'tongue in cheek' fashion amongst both sexes for black leather or vinyl 'Kinky' gear.

SLEEVE OF THE BEATLES SECOND LP
WITH THE BEATLES, BRITISH, 1963

The sleeve of the Beatles second album, which dispensed with the Fab Four's bright and chirpy persona in favour of a dramatically-lit, somewhat dour, grainy black-and-white portrait of the group by the photographer Robert Freeman, was quite unlike that of any Pop album before. Brian Epstein, the group's manager, commissioned Freeman for the cover portrait, after seeing a series of stark black-and-white photographs of Modern Jazz musicians, amongst them John Coltrane, which Freeman had taken for the *Sunday Times*. The sombre image is indicative of the group's future ambitions, implying that they were due the respect then accorded to well-known Jazz musicians, and suggesting that, after the juvenile excitement surrounding them earlier that year, they were here to stay and should be taken seriously. The sleeve has since become one of the most memorable and enduring images of the Beatles.

CHANGE OF ADDRESS CARD
PETER GEE, ANGLO-AMERICAN
1963

The Pop artist and graphic designer Peter Gee moved from London to New York in 1963, where he met with great professional success. Soon after arriving in the city, he cleverly enlarged the envelopes of several letters he'd received from friends in Britain onto a large surreal scale, similar to Claes Oldenberg sculptures, which he sent out in true Pop fashion as 'change of address' cards.

POST EARLY
IN
THE DAY.

LONDON N.W.
6 45 PM
2 NOV
1963
B

POSTAGE REVENUE
1'3

x. Peter Gee

506 West Broadway

New York

12 N. Y

U. S. A.

SWINGING SIXTIES 1964–1967

SLEEVE OF LP RECORD, READY, STEADY, GO!
BRITISH, 1964

Independent Television's new youth programme,' Ready, Steady, Go! ', produced by Associated-Rediffusion, was launched in August 1963, and ran until December 1966. With its catchphrase, 'The weekend starts here', it became essential viewing for Britain's 'Mod' youth on Friday evenings, with the latest dances and 'Mod' fashions on view, and the latest Pop singles performed by groups like the Beatles and the Rolling Stones. In 1963, the early shows were presented by Dusty Springfield, but from 1964 by Cathy McGowan, who, for a time, became the face of 'Mod' Britain. The programme's influence was incalculable in spreading Pop culture across the country and far beyond. The design of this sleeve for the first, Ready, Steady, Go! compilation forms, more or less, a survey of some of the new British Pop groups which changed Pop and its culture forever.

SILK-SCREENED BORDER PRINT TEXTILE, HARRY GORDON (ATTRIB), BRITISH, 1965

This textile, used here for the aprons worn by hostesses and waitresses at the opening of the revamped 'Ready Steady Goes Live' show in April 1965, would have also been used for mini-dresses and other garments worn at the event. Gordon subsequently used screen-printed photographic images for his range of 'Poster' dresses in 1967, and in 1968 adapted the logo used here for the new Cinecenta cinema complex in Panton Street, London.

Although not among the outfits she eventually wore in the movie, this jacket was included in a group of highly fashionable items selected in 1966 for Audrey Hepburn to wear in the British film, *Two For The Road*. Both jacket and coat are the acme of British Pop fashion in the 1960s.

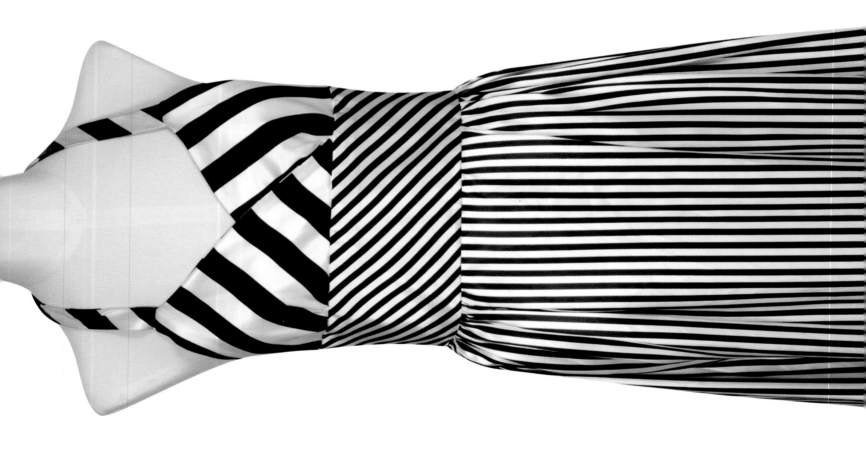

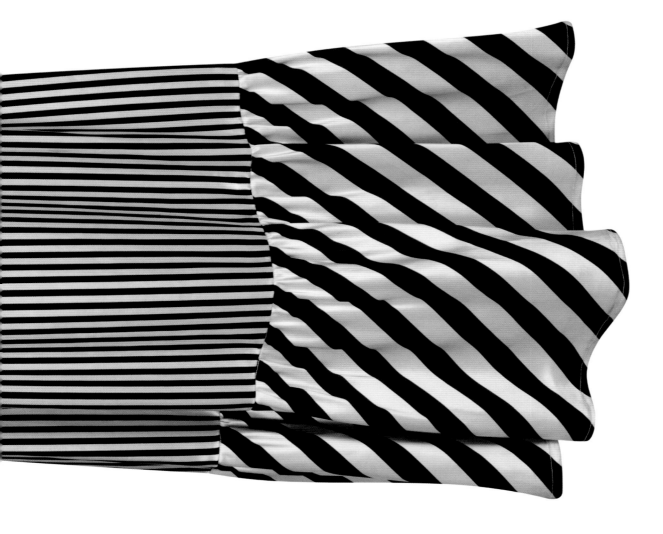

'OP' SATIN EVENING DRESS
MARY QUANT FOR THE GINGER
GROUP RANGE, BRITISH, c1965

Quant set up the Ginger Group label in 1963 as a relatively inexpensive fashion range aimed at the youth market. It was one of the most accessible and influential innovations in Pop fashion.

DARK BLUE AND WHITE STRIPED COTTON
'OP' MINI-DRESS, MARY QUANT
BRITISH, c1966

This simple shift dress, a standard item in most girls wardrobes in the later 1960s, is an early example of a Quant mini-dress, in which she makes clever play with a simple striped fabric to achieve a strong visual effect.

DARK BLUE AND WHITE STRIPED COTTON JACKET, BIBA, BRITISH, c1967

Like Mary Quant, Barbara Hulanicki (founder of Biba), also created a powerful 'Op' effect for this jacket by the clever and imaginative cutting of a simple fabric.

This shoulder bag is one of Quant's first two designs for women's bags. The design is an early version of her famous 'Daisy' logo.

These boots were inspired both by 'Op' art and the style of the white leather boots designed by André Courrèges for his 'Space Age' collection of 1964-65.

Jane Birkin played one of the two young models who appeared with the actor David Hemmings in the well-known scene, set in his photographic studio, in the film *Blow Up*, the film director Antonioni's classic depiction of 'Swinging London'. In this portrait by the iconic fashion photographer David Bailey, Birkin, wearing an 'Op' inspired dress, and holding a black and white target brooch to her eye, epitomises 'Mod' style. The brooch was from a range of 'Op' jewellery available from the King's Road boutique, Top Gear, one of the most exclusive 'mod' boutiques, and the one of which Barbara Hulanicki (Biba) was most envious. The 'bull's-eye' motif became particularly associated with Top Gear who used it on their 'tote' bags and other packaging. (Photograph of Jane Birkin courtesy David Bailley)

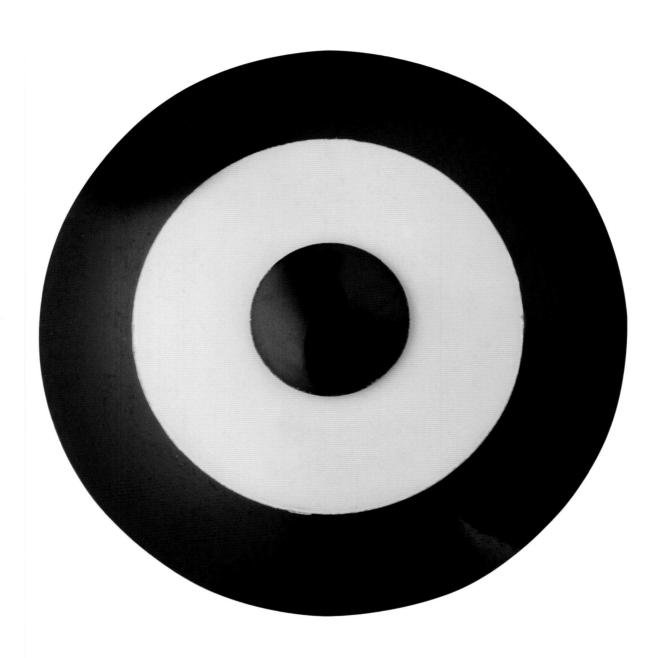

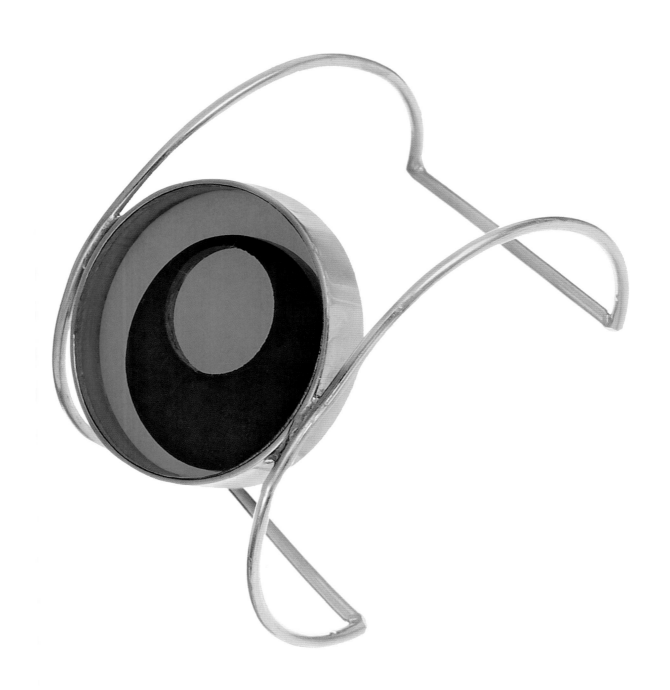

Manchester United player 'Georgie' Best was Britain's first football superstar, the 1960s equivalent of today's David Beckham. Endowed with exceptional talent as a player, a model's good looks, great charisma and a wacky personal charm, he was nicknamed by the press, the fifth Beatle. Early in 1966, he capitalized on his name and fame by setting up a unisex fashion boutique with a Manchester City player, Mike Summerbee, in the Sale area of Greater Manchester, close to the Old Trafford ground of Manchester United.

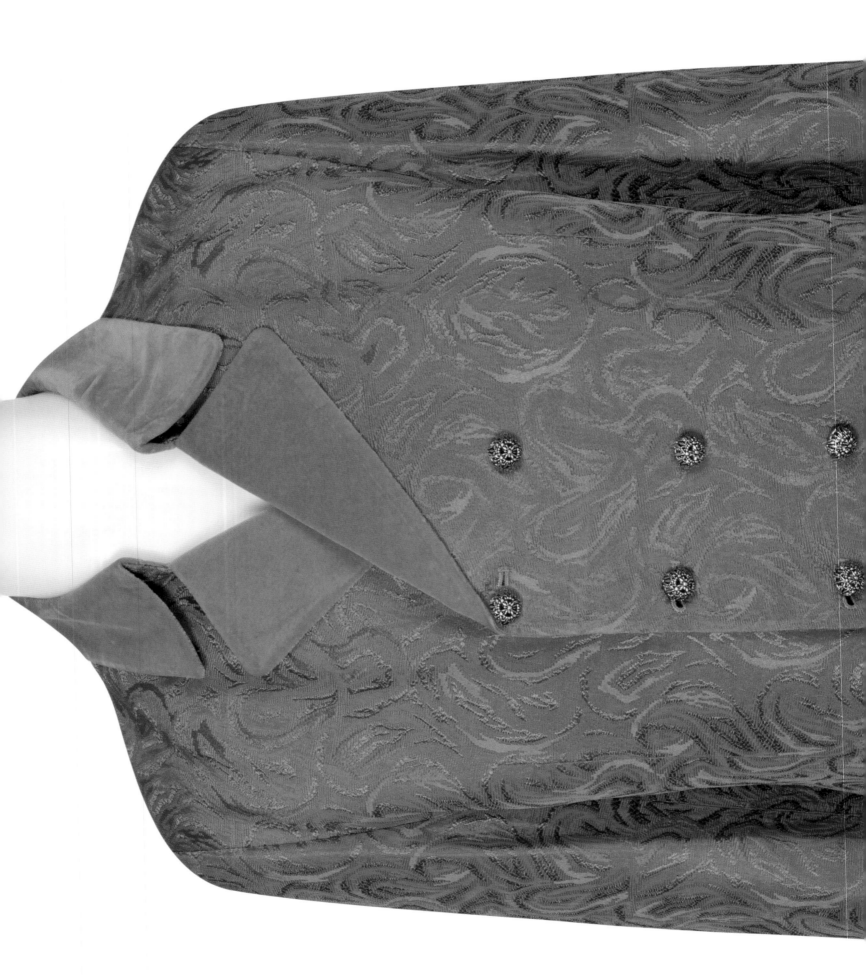

MAN'S BROCADE DANDY JACKET, TAKE 6, BRITISH, c1967

Take 6 was an extremely successful male boutique in London's Carnaby Street. Aimed at the middle-range market, it allowed many young men access to high styled dandy fashions, which were otherwise only available at much more expensive and exclusive male boutiques. This particular jacket in brocade and velvet, epitomises the dandy style of 'Swinging London'.

Between 1965 and 1966, the Anglo-American Pop artist and graphic designer Peter Gee designed the logo and packaging for Paraphernalia, New York's first 'Mod' fashion boutique. Betsey Johnson, Paraphernalia's principal designer, was a good friend of Gee's, and he silk-screened the various pieces of packaging with images of her and her friend, the model Penelope Tree.

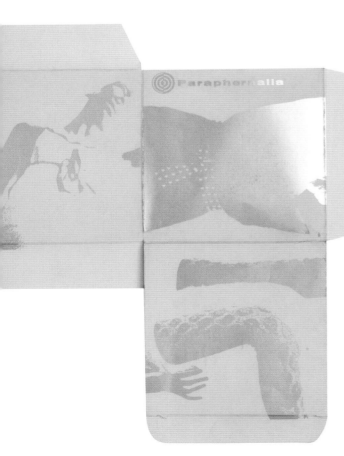

DRESS WITH AN APPLIQUE DESIGN OF THE
PARAPHERNALIA LOGO, MICHAEL MOTT
FOR PARAPHERNALIA, AMERICAN, c1966

Michael Mott was one of the original team of talented young fashion designers who worked for
Paraphernalia under the direction of Betsey Johnson. Following her departure in 1968, Mott took over her
role as the boutique's principal designer.

DRESS WITH A DESIGN OF APPLIQUED
ARROWS, LESLIE JUNIORS
AMERICAN, c1966

Specifically designed for the teenage market, this dress shows both the influence of the Paraphernalia style, and 'Hard Edged Abstraction', which, with 'Op' art, was one of the major artistic influences on Pop fashion in the mid-1960s.

This dress, with its design influenced by 'Op' and 'Hard Edged Abstraction', is from Hanae Mori's first couture collection, 'East meets West', which she launched in New York in 1965. The collection proved so successful that she subsequently opened two boutiques in the city. The doyenne of post-war Japanese couture, her work prepared the way for the success of later Japanese fashion designers such as Kansai Yamamoto and Issey Miyake. A dress of this design was owned by the Queen's younger sister, Princess Margaret, in the mid-1960s.

Between 1963 and 1967, boots, the antithesis of the fragile and elegant stiletto-heeled shoe, became the most fashionable footwear for young women. No longer an item of heavy duty wear, they came in a wide variety of styles and materials, but nowhere more so than in America. These plastic Mondrian boots were inspired by a brief fashion in 1966 for clothing in the style of Mondrian's paintings, designed by the French couturier Yves Saint Laurent. The 'Glo Glo' boots, in a plasticsized cotton material with a luminous green stripe, were the ultimate footware in discotheques.

The imagery of this remarkable scarf epitomises London's Pop culture in the mid 1960s. Although a somewhat risqué item for an upmarket store like Liberty to produce, even the most conservative of retail establishments eased their stays a little in the giddy atmosphere of the time.

The designer, Colin Fulcher, (Barney Bubbles), was one of the most influential and gifted British graphic designers of the 1960s and 1970s. The Muleskinners, a Rhythm and Blues group, was formed in 1963 by Ian Mclagan (Little Mac), a student at Twickenham Art School, who was later keyboardist with the Small Faces. Fulcher, slightly older than Little Mac, also studied at Twickenham, and, like other students there, was a regular of the Eel Pie Island Club, a well known Rhythm and Blues and Jazz venue, located opposite the town on an island in the Thames. In late 1963, following a short Rolling Stones residency, the Muleskinners often played when the main band on the bill, such as Long John Baldry and the Hoochie Coochie Men, 'took five'. The club was a gathering place for many future 1960s stars who were also former students of local art schools, such as Tom McGuinness, a member of the Manfred Mann group, Eric Clapton, Pete Townshend, and fellow traveller Rod Stewart. It is a perfect example of the way the subtle interconnections between art schools, Pop musicians and Pop designers facilitated the growth of Pop culture. This promotional poster for the Muleskinners received a Design award in 1965.

DRESS AND CLOTHES HANGER FROM THE 'TWIGGY DRESSES' COLLECTION, BRITISH c1966. BADGE, 'FORGET OXFAM FEED TWIGGY', BRITISH, LATE 1960S

Like George Best, the 1960s teenage supermodel, Twiggy, (Lesley Hornby) capitalised on her sudden fame in 1966 by launching a range of clothing under her name. Although the designs, aimed at the youth market, were the work of two young graduates of the Royal College of Art, Pamela Proctor and Paul Babb, their brief required them to work closely with Twiggy, as all the designs had to receive her personal approval. Each item in the range was sold with a cleverly-designed hanger printed with her face. The badge is a satirical comment on Twiggy's near-emaciated appearance, the origin of her professional name.

MAN'S BLAZER, JOHN STEPHEN, BRITISH, c1965

The Edwardian blazer was revived as appropriate wear for the elegant dandies of mid-60s London, and Pete Townshend and Keith Moon of The Who were frequently photographed wearing them. This example in red, white and blue is from the John Stephen boutique, Carnaby Street.

In the mid-60s members of The Who often wore clothing made from Union Jacks, as on this record sleeve. 1965 saw the emergence of the Union Jack flag as a Pop motif, an ironic symbol of 'Swinging' London. Once the focus of patriotic pride, actual flags were irreverently made up into jackets and waistcoats, often to the scandal of more conventional tourists. The Union Jack was also screen-printed onto fabric for mini dresses, and used to decorate mugs and tin ware. Following the devaluation of the pound in 1967, a further irony came with the British establishment's subversion of this iconoclastic use of the flag, when Harold Wilson's Labour government co-opted it for their 'I'm Backing Britain' campaign.

MINI DRESS MADE FROM A RAYON FABRIC,
SILK SCREEN-PRINTED WITH A PATTERN OF
UNION JACKS, CARNABY STREET BRITISH, c1966

WAISTCOAT MADE FROM A UNION JACK FLAG WITH
ORIGINAL MILITARY BUTTONS, BRITISH, c1965-66
POSSIBLY CREATED FOR EITHER OF THE BOUTIQUES
DODO OR I WAS LORD KITCHENER'S VALET

'BRITISH RUBBISH' BINS, SCREEN-PRINTED TIN
DODO, BRITAIN, 1965

Like paper, screen-printed tin was used extensively by British Pop designers for its versatile low-cost, throwaway qualities. These 'British Rubbish' bins for the Pop boutique Dodo were an amusing ironic comment on imperialism, nationalism, patriotism and militarism.

Paul Clark was a leading Pop designer in the 'Swinging London' era, whose work was particularly popular in the boutiques of London's Carnaby Street. The name of the boutique, I was Lord Kitchener's Valet, was taken from that of a First World War British general, whose image was used by Clark for the design of this mug, an ironic comment on the futility of war and mindless patriotism. The use of Kitchener's image was further extended with the hugely popular reprint of the military recruiting poster 'Your Country Needs You'. For the design of this plate, Clark used a 'target' motif, another dynamic symbol of the era, derived originally from the American artist Jasper Johns's series of target paintings, which the British painter Peter Blake subsequently developed in the early 1960s as a Pop painting, 'The First Real Target'. The sharp geometric clarity of both the Union Jack and the target fitted well with the mid-1960s vogue for design derived from Op' art and 'Hard Edged Abstraction'.

The remarkable dial of this 'Revolutionary Clock', was originally designed by Paul Clark c1966 for Perspective Designs, who used it with a variety of stands. This slightly later example is in a simple white acrylic case, designed by Anthony Gemmill for Acrylic Designs, c1968.

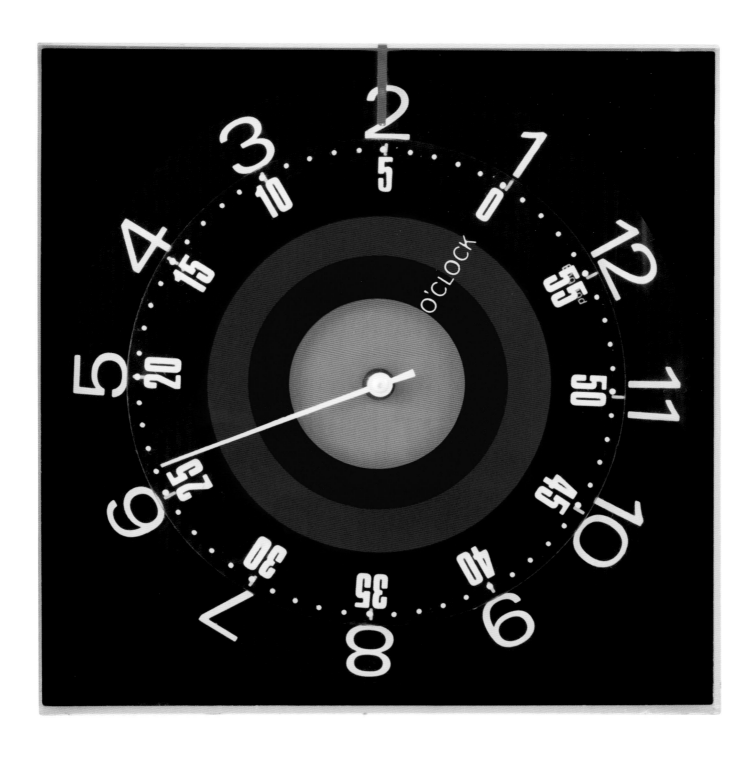

COFFEE SERVICE, 'CORSETS', SUSAN WILLIAMS-ELLIS
FOR PORTMERION POTTERY, BRITISH, 1965

This coffee service is an excellent example of the amusing and, sometimes, slightly risqué use of Victorian advertisements for Pop design.

STORAGE TIN, 'SALOME' FOR JRM DESIGNS
IAN LOGAN, BRITISH, 1967

In 1967 the packaging designer Ian Logan began to produce a highly acclaimed series of screen-printed storage tins for his company, JRM Designs, among them 'Lollipop', 1968 and, the following year, 'Harriet'. In 1969 this particular design, 'Salome', was voted by readers of the Observer newspaper to be the 'Antique of 2001'.

'KNOCK-DOWN' CHAIR C1, SCHOFIELD AND WRIGHT, BRITISH, 1964. STILL FROM THE FILM *BLOW UP*, 1967

Designed to be sold in flat packs, 'knock-down' furniture had a vogue in the mid- to late-1960s. Inexpensive to produce (in theory) and easily disposable, it fitted well with the notion of throwaway Pop design. Jean Schofield and John Wright developed this particular chair while students at the Royal College of Art. Although low tech and low cost to manufacture, its advanced concept and radical appearance resulted in very few being produced. These were sold through an exclusive retail outlet, Anderson Manson Decorations of London, for the, then, not inconsiderable price of £45.10s – (£45.50). In 1966 the chair received the accolade of being chosen for the set of the photographer's studio in *Blow Up*, Antonioni's definitive movie of 'Swinging' London. (Film still courtesy of Philippe Garner Collection)

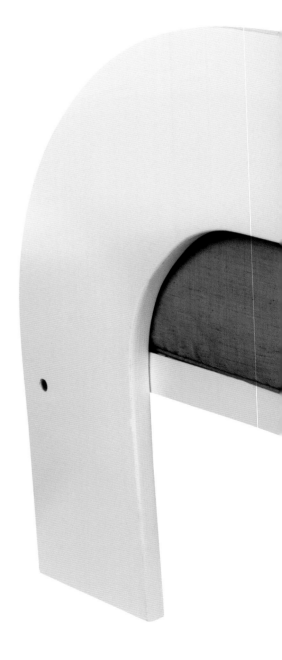

Anthony Graham Designs, based in the Blackheath area of London, specialised in the manufacture of inexpensive knock-down furniture made from simple cut-out flat sheets of spray-painted plywood and lengths of dowelling. A range of knock-down children's furniture, designed for the company by Anthony Gooding, was selected for the Design Council Index in 1968 and featured in the January 1969 issue of *Design* magazine. This earlier adult-size chair was, probably, also designed by Gooding.

Transparent inflatable furniture was another inexpensive Pop throwaway fashionable in the late 1960s. This 'Aire Chair', by the British company, Associated Industrial Designs, was marketed as 'A new concept in casual decor' which 'goes everywhere anytime!' Compared to that of most other inflatable chairs, its design is highly original, and the opaque covering a move away from the transparent plastic then generally used to give a 'Space Age' look.

Produced between 1964 and 1966 by the American company, the International Paper Corporation Inc., this child's chair was the first piece of paper furniture. Stamped out as a piece of flat card at one per second, for a cost of a few pence per unit, eight hundred could be stacked and stored in a pile four feet high, before being folded for use, like a piece of origami. The chair's life expectancy was between three to six months. It retailed in Britain for thirty shillings (£2.50).

A paper table from Peter Murdoch's second range of children's furniture 'One of Those Things', the decorative pattern designed by Paul Clark.

This is the first successful paper chair designed for adults. It was manufactured from 1967 by Thames Board Mills, and retailed for forty five shillings (£2.25).

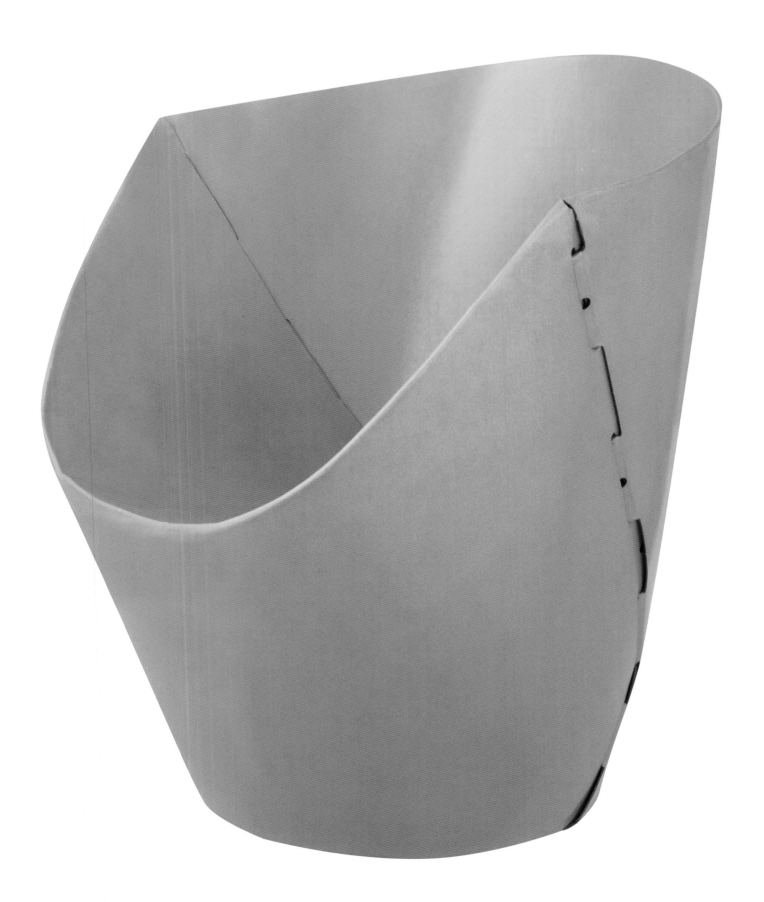

The ultimate Pop throwaway, the paper dress, originated in America in 1966, when the Scott Paper Company launched their 'Paper Caper' dress as a promotion for a new reinforced paper product. To the company's surprise it proved a runaway success and by the end of the year they had sold nearly half a million dresses. The fad reached its apogee in 1967, when the British designer Harry Gordon launched his range of 'Poster' dresses. He initially produced five designs with photographic images, including the one illustrated here, a blow-up of Audrey Hepburn's eye. His intention was to produce a new dress every week, each with an image of a different Pop star. In the event, he never got beyond the first, an image of Bob Dylan, who objected so vehemently that Gordon was obliged to withdraw it from sale.

POSTER DRESS

PAPER CLOCK, 'ARABESQUE C2', PAUL CLARK FOR
PERSPECTIVE DESIGNS LTD, BRITISH, 1968

'POLY LION', A SELF-ASSEMBLY PAPERBOARD GIFT BOX
CLIFF RICHARDS FOR GOODS AND CHATTELS
BRITISH, 1968

The British Pop designer Cliff Richards was a member of the Polypops Design Studio, set up in 1967 with the backing of the Polycell Company. Richards had previously created a successful series of pop-up Pop cards in 1965 for Gear of Carnaby Street, and the following year the 'Slottizoo' range of paper animals. He subsequently designed a well-known 'Polypops' range for Paperchase, which included wrapping paper, paper dolls houses and screen-printed tin trays.

The ubiquitous paper carrier bag was elevated in the mid 1960s to the status of a high fashion accessory, when Pop designers such as Cliff Richards and Paul Clark created colourful witty designs for this humble mundane object, renamed the 'tote' bag.

TWO PROTOTYPE PAPER TOTE BAGS AND PACKAGING
PETER GEE, ANGLO-AMERICAN, c1967

Gee designed these tote bags and packaging for DuPont, the developers of nylon textiles. The witty and sexual connotations of the slogan, 'Touch, it feels different because it is', was used in combination with images of attractive young girls to hopefully suggest the potential pleasures afforded by the sensual and erotic qualities of nylon!

PAPER TOTE BAG, 'CAMPBELL'S SOUP CAN'
ANDY WARHOL, AMERICAN, 1966

Warhol used his iconic image of a Campbell's tomato soup can for this tote bag, which he designed to be sold during the exhibition of his work, 'Andy Warhol', held at the Institute of Contemporary Art, Boston, in 1966.

'Something Special', the second range of jewellery by Wendy Ramshaw and her husband the sculptor David Watkins, were ephemeral throwaway paper items, sold in do-it-yourself flat packs. Ramshaw went on to become one of the most internationally-important contemporary jewellers, and Watkins, Professor of Silversmithing, Jewellery and Metalwork at the Royal College of Art.

Gee's great interest in colour theories, such as that of Joseph Albers, or the 'Hard Edge Abstraction' of Barnett Newman, are very evident in the designs of these storage boxes.

These clothes hangers with images of John Lennon and Jimi Hendix were part of a range of hangers with images of Pop and film stars, such as Faye Dunaway, and David Hemmings, star of the iconic 1960s films, *Blow Up* and *Barbarella*.

MANUFACTURED EXCLUSIVELY BY SAUNDERS ENTERPRISES   JIMMI HENDRIX

PAPER 133

TWO PAPER MOBILES, 'HANG-UM-UPS', SCM ALLIED
PAPER INCORPORATED, AMERICAN, c1967

These two mobiles, entitled 'Love' and 'Peace', exemplify the overarching sentiment of youth during San Francisco's 1967 Summer of Love.

TWO GREETINGS CARDS, JAN PIENKOWSKI
FOR GALLERY FIVE, BRITISH, c1968

These greetings cards are some of the earliest 'non occasion' cards without any printed message. One of the cards has an image of the silent movie star, Theda Bara, well known at the time in Britain, as her image was then used for the logo of the Underground newspaper, the *International Times*. The other card has an image of Warren Beatty, as the 1930s gangster, Clyde Barrow, in the 1967 film *Bonnie and Clyde*.

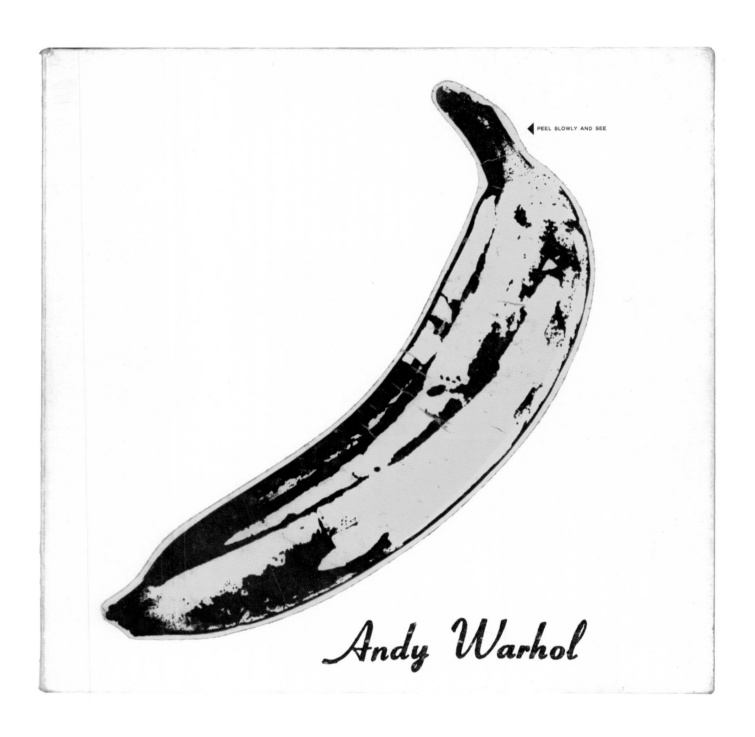

PEEL SLOWLY AND SEE

Andy Warhol

In 1965, Andy Warhol took over management of The Velvet Underground, thought by many to be the most influential band of the decade. He designed the sleeve of their first album, *The Velvet Underground and Nico*, for which he used a peelable yellow banana covering a pink one. It is considered the most iconic of his record sleeves.

THROWAWAY PAPER PLATE, ROY LICHTENSTEIN
AMERICAN, 1969

This paper plate was commissioned from the Pop artist Roy Lichtenstein in 1969 by the photographer Bert Stern for his store, 'On 1st', in New York. It was a short-lived venture which closed soon after this plate was produced. Stern was the photographer who, shortly before her death in 1962, took the 'Last Sitting' photographs of Marilyn Monroe. He later photographed many 1960s icons, such as the supermodels Jean Shrimpton and Twiggy, and the movie stars Audrey Hepburn and Brigitte Bardot.

WALLPAPER, 'RIGHT HAND LADY', ALLEN JONES BRITISH, 1972

'Right Hand Lady' was commissioned from the Pop artist Allen Jones by the German wallpaper manufacturer Marburger Tapenfabrik, for their 1972 'X Art Wall' collection. Work by the Pop artists Peter Phillips and Niki de Saint Phalle was also included in the collection.

PAPER 'HIPPY' WALL MIRROR, AMERICAN, c1967

The 'Hippy' image of this clever wall mirror personifies San Francisco's 1967 'Summer of Love'. The mirrored sun shades were influenced by a poster in Victor Moscoso's 'Neon Rose' series, for a Chambers Brothers gig at the San Francisco venue, The Matrix, and Richard Avedon's psychedelic poster of John Lennon, both from 1967. It is essentially a transitional object between the throwaway culture of 'Swinging London', and the more ethically concerned counter-culture, then beginning to emerge in San Francisco.

PSYCHEDELIA
1967–1970

TUNIC TOP, SONNY AND CHER
AMERICAN, c1966

In 1966, the Pop duo, Sonny and Cher gave their name to a line of clothing, which they either designed themselves, or in conjunction with the fashion designer Carol Brent. The range was mainly sold through the Montgomery Ward chain of department stores. A departure from London's 'Mod' style, then universally fashionable with the young, the Sonny and Cher range was a particularly early commercial manifestation of the American West Coast 'Hippy' look.

MAN'S KAFTAN, THE SCOTT LESTER ORGANISATION BRITISH, c1967

The Beatle's brief encounter with the Indian guru Maharishi Mahesh Yogi in the 'Summer of Love', attracted great publicity when they donned Indian garb for a short while. Thereafter, a vaguely eastern exoticisim became the vogue amongst both young 'Hippy' seekers of enlightenment and their more fashion conscious contemporaries. This commercially-manufactured man's kaftan is made in a psychedelic-influenced textile in the style of the nineteenth-century designer William Morris.

MEN'S EMBROIDERED SHOES, INDIAN, c1967

This pair of mens shoes would have been made in India as a one-off commission for someone on the 'Hippy' trail. India was then still a land of craftsmen, and such commissions were easily given, quickly completed and inexpensively made. The uppers are of extremely fine leather, beautifully embroidered with Indian chain stitch.

MINI-SKIRT, GRANNY TAKES A TRIP, BRITISH, 1967

The London boutique, Granny Takes A Trip, was set up in February 1966 by the graphic designer Nigel Waymouth, his girlfriend Sheila Cohen and the tailor John Pearse, who was responsible for the boutique's more finely-tailored garments in interesting fabrics. Many of the jackets, dresses and skirts – such as the one illustrated here – were made in Arts and Crafts textiles designed by William Morris, and other nineteenth-century designers such as Lindsey Butterfield, which chimed well with the psychedelic aesthetic fashionable at the time. The boutique also pioneered the selling of authentic Victorian and Edwardian clothing. Early outfits by 'Granny' are worn by the Beatles on the back cover of their LP, *Revolver*, and the Rolling Stones on the cover of their LP, *Between the Buttons*.

ABOVE: LP RECORD SLEEVE, THE FOOL, ANGLO-DUTCH, 1968

This LP record sleeve demonstrates the close interconnectedness which existed between Pop music and Pop design. The Fool design collective had created clothing and graphics for the Beatles Apple Store and, previously, costumes and record sleeves for the Hollies and Cream. Indeed, the former Hollies musician Graham Nash – later of Crosby, Stills, Nash and Young – was the producer of The Fool's LP.

RIGHT: POSTER, 'GRANNY TAKES A TRIP', HAPSHASH AND THE COLOURED COAT BRITISH, 1968

A promotional poster for Granny Takes A Trip, by its proprietor Nigel Waymouth and the graphic designer Michael English, who worked together as Hapshash and the Coloured Coat. Other than Martin Sharp of Oz, they were the most influential graphic artists of the British counter-culture.

SCREEN PRINTED COTTON FURNISHING TEXTILE, 'SWITCH ON 70'
BERNARD WARDLE LTD, BRITISH, 1969

This textile was produced to mark the beginning of the new decade. Its psychedelic erotism is derived from films and comic book fantasies such as *Barbarella*, *Modesty Blaise* and, even more so, Guy Peellaert's comic book character, Pravda. Although a furnishing textile, the designer Eddie Pond suggests the soft cotton fabric used indicates it was probably also intended for bed linen and quilt covers.

SCREEN PRINTED COTTON FURNISHING TEXTILE
'LOVE AND PEACE', CONCORD FABRICS
AMERICAN, c1967

The New York textile company, Concord Fabrics, produced a number of significant Pop textiles in the late 1960s and early 1970s, including this one, redolent of the 'Summer of Love'. Another of Concord's Pop textiles, a dress fabric, 'Love Comic' by Leon Rosenblatt, was subsequently included in the Victoria and Albert Museum's 1974 exhibition, 'The Fabric of Pop'.

SCREEN-PRINTED COTTON FURNISHING TEXTILE 'CURTAIN UP', SHIRLEY CRAVEN, HULL TRADERS BRITISH, 1970

Like 'Switch On 70', this textile was possibly intended to herald the new decade. The symmetrical design – which conjures up a pair of psychedelic stage curtains, reminiscent of classic Rorschach ink blots – is realised in an 'Acid' drenched palette similar to that of the Beatles animated movie, *The Yellow Submarine*, or the psychedelic experience associated with LSD trips.

LP RECORD SLEEVE, *DISRAELI GEARS*
MARTIN SHARP, ANGLO-AUSTRALIAN, 1967

The sleeve for the first LP of the British super-group Cream is the work of Martin Sharp, co-founder and art director of *Oz* magazine. Through his remarkable art work for *Oz*, Sharp became the most influential graphic designer of the British counter-culture. Here he successfully conveys the power of Cream's music through the dynamic design of this iconic psychedelic sleeve.

POSTER, 'LOVE', PETER MAX
AMERICAN, 1968

Peter Max is probably the best known of American Pop graphic designers. This poster, his most celebrated image, dates from the year before he became a household name in 1969, following an eight page feature on his work in *Life* magazine, for which he also appeared on the cover.

DENIM JACKET, MARTIN BERNARD LTD, INTERNATIONAL
FASHIONS, 1971. BADGES, BRITISH AND AMERICAN,
1964-1974. INSET, BADGE BY ROBERT CRUMB.
OPPOSITE: PORTRAIT OF THE PHOTOGRAPHER
MICHAEL COOPER FROM *THE BOX OF PINUPS*,
DAVID BAILEY, BRITISH, 1965

Long ubiquitous in America, by the late 1960s denim clothing was an essential part of the wardrobe of most 'Cool' young people, 'Hippies' or not. Although plain and functional, it provided an ideal vehicle for radical forms of decoration. Of these the wearing of inexpensive throwaway tin badges was the most immediate; an instant and infinitely variable form of self-expression, whose subject matter, from Rock bands to the Vietnam War, was largely rooted in the 'counter-culture'. (Photograph of Michael Cooper courtesy of David Bailey)

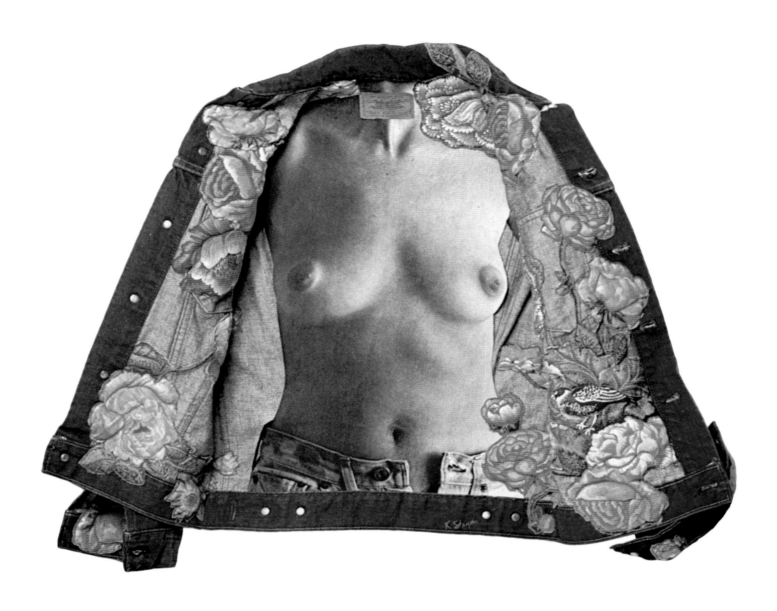

INTERIOR AND EXTERIOR OF A DECORATED DENIM JACKET, KAY SHUPER, AMERICAN, EARLY 1970S

The decoration of denim with embroidery and various forms of appliqué originated in the late 1960s environment of San Francisco's 'Hippy' counter-culture, where it became an elevated form of urban folk art. The fashion quickly spread internationally, but soon degenerated in a flood of commercially-produced cheap machine embroidered denim clothing and appliqué 'patches'. However, the high level of artistry and technical skill used for the jacket illustrated here indicates that it was a one-off piece, almost certainly the work of a professional designer and embroiderer.

EMBROIDERED AND APPLIQUÉD DENIM WAISTCOAT
MOONBEAM, AMERICAN, c1971

Commissioned for the Pop star Elton John, this finely-embroidered waistcoat is an exquisite example of American West Coast denim art. The decorations are metaphors for concepts dear to the counter-culture: ruralism, a oneness with nature, the return to the land, and the idealised comfort of a simple home and hearth. The image of a seal pup personifies the 'Save the Seals' campaign of the late 1960s, the first of many such responses by the burgeoning ecological movement. The ensemble is completed with a badge depicting a grazing cow, inspired by the sleeve of Pink Floyd's 1970 album, Atom Heart Mother, by the British design group Hipgnosis.

SCREEN-PRINTED DENIM TEXTILE, CONCORD FABRICS, AMERICAN, c1969. A PAIR OF JEANS IN THE SAME FABRIC, c1969

Printed denim became extremely popular in the late 1960s. One of the first is this remarkable textile by Concord Fabrics, screen-printed with a photographic image of the crowds at the fabled 1969 Woodstock Festival. Billed as 'An Aquarian Exposition: Three Days of Peace and Music', it has since become the template for all future Rock festivals. Woodstock was a high point in Pop culture, with legendary performances from some of the greatest Rock and Pop stars and bands, such as Jimi Hendrix, Santana and Janis Joplin, before crowds of some 500,000. Concord fabrics quickly realised the historic and cultural significance of the event, and soon after produced this textile, which was used for a variety of denim clothing, such as the jeans illustrated here.

LP RECORD SLEEVE, ANDY WARHOL WITH CRAIG BRAUN FOR THE ROLLING STONES ALBUM, *STICKY FINGERS*
AMERICAN, 1970

Warhol's sleeve for *Sticky Fingers* features the jean-clad lower torso of a well-endowed young man, whose fly, complete with a real working zip, opens to reveals his underwear. The back of the sleeve has the young man's rear printed on it. Warhol carried out the photography for the sleeve with the help of his studio assistant and former lover Billy Name (William Linich), using various young men as models, some of whom were boyfriends. However, he would never confirm whose image he finally used. It was the designer Craig Braun who actually realised Warhol's concept for the sleeve.

LONG SLEEVED T-SHIRT, 'CHE GUEVARA', BRITISH, c1970

In the late 1960s, T-shirts worn with jeans became an essential, inexpensive but fashionable unisex uniform for many radical young people involved in the counter-culture. The T-shirt particularly allowed plenty of scope for self expression, as it could be instantly transformed with 'on the spot' transfer-printed designs from an apparently endless variety of slogans and images, the most popular being of the romantic Cuban revolutionary hero, Che Guevara. Following Che's dramatic capture and execution in Bolivia in 1967, the Irish graphic artist Jim Fitzpatrick created a high contrast monochrome graphic portrait of him in 1968, which almost immediately became an international icon, the ultimate symbol of political struggle and protest, universally applied to posters, flags, and T-shirts .

UNDERGROUND POSTERS & GRAPHICS 1966–1973

POSTER POEM, 'SEX, WAR, SEX, CARS'. DEREK BOSHIER AND CHRISTOPHER LOGUE, GEAR OF CARNABY STREET, BRITISH, 1966

Between 1966 and 1967, the poet Christopher Logue created a series of Poster Poems, some in conjunction by the Pop artist Derek Boshier. They were produced by Vandal Productions for the boutique, Gear of Carnaby Street. This is a particularly early example of an anti-Vietnam War poster.

PROMOTIONAL POSTER FOR 'IT'
THE INTERNATIONAL TIMES NEWSPAPER
BRITISH, c1966

The principal news sheet of the British 'underground press', the *International Times*, 'IT', was set up in 1966. An image of the silent movie star Theda Bara was accidently chosen for the paper's logo, when the staff mistook her for Clara Bow, the original 1920s 'IT girl'. However Bara's image become so identified with the paper it was decided to retain it.

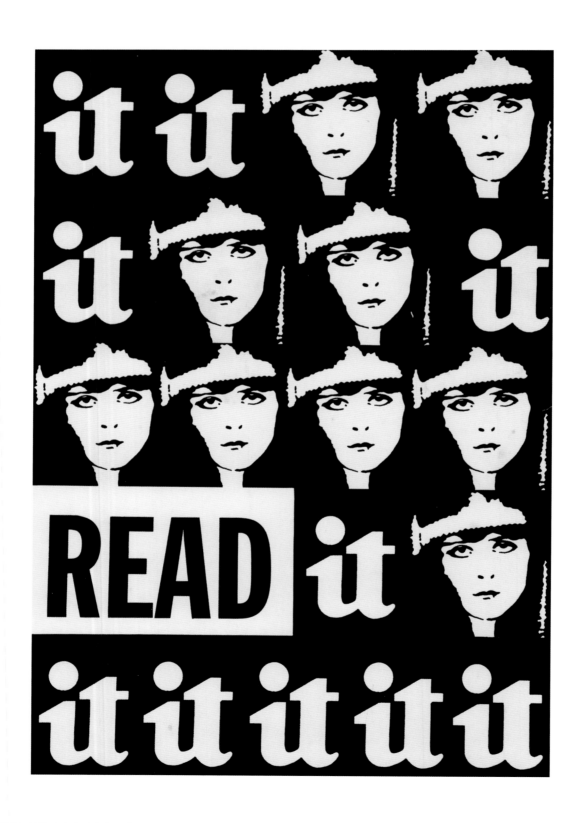

'IT' NO. 92, NOVEMBER 19 – DECEMBER 3
BRITISH, 1970

Shortly after the first issue the London *Times* threatened litigation over the publication's title, which the publisher then abbreviated to 'IT'. Many celebrated members of the counter-culture became contributors to the paper, among them Germaine Greer, John Peel, William Burroughs and Allen Ginsberg.

The satirical magazine *Oz* was first published in Sidney, Australia, in 1963. The magazine's founders, Richard Neville and Martin Sharp, moved to London in 1966, where, between 1967 and 1973, they produced the magazine as a subversive 'underground' publication. The co-editors in London were Jim Anderson and Felix Dennis. The most successful and influential publication of the British 'underground press', its remarkable graphic style, the result of Martin Sharp's dynamic art direction, attracted some of the most talented graphic designers and artists involved with the counter-culture. All designed covers and art work for it, amongst them the graphic designers Barney Bubbles (Colin Fulcher), Hapshash and The Coloured Coat, and the American satirist and cartoonist Robert Crumb.

OZ, 'SCHOOL KIDS' ISSUE, NO. 28, BRITISH, MAY 1970

The May 1970 issue of *Oz* was handed over to twenty secondary school kids to edit without any interference. The result was catastrophic for the *Oz* editors who were charged under the 1959 obscenity laws with producing an obscene publication and conspiring to corrupt public morals. By trying them, many felt the Establishment were out to prosecute the counter-culture itself. Opposition to the trial grew in strength, with John Lennon and Yoko Ono joining protest marches and the artist David Hockney producing a print of the *Oz* editors naked, to raise funds for their defence. The court's verdict, considered a foregone conclusion by many, found the defendants guilty, who were then imprisoned, where, despite awaiting the outcome of an appeal, their long hair was cut in an act calculated to humiliate them. Amidst the ensuing outcry they were subsequently found not guilty at the appeal hearing.

INK, 'UNDERGROUND' NEWS SHEET FRONT PAGE, 'OZ NOT GUILTY', ISSUE NO. 15, BRITISH, AUGUST 1971

Ink, launched in April 1971, was more overtly political than other 'underground' newspapers and magazines. The concept of its founder and editor Richard Neville, also the editor of *Oz*, was to link the 'underground' with the 'overground' press. It was a short-lived enterprise which folded soon after the *Oz* trial in Febuary 1972. The satirical cartoon on this front page, by Ralph Steadman, is of the trial's judge, Michael Argyle.

COVER OF 'ACID' OZ 'SEX FAIR SPECIAL' NO.27, APRIL 1970

This cover for *Oz* is by the leading American 'underground' cartoonist and graphic artist Robert Crumb, whose searing Rabelaisian satires were a major influence on the publications of the international counter-culture. The cover's image, a savage parody of a self portrait, is signed 'Cover Boy Crumb'.

FLY POSTER FOR THE FRENCH 'UNDERGROUND' PUBLICATION L'ACTUEL, 'UNDERGROUND, OU VAS – TU?', ROBERT CRUMB c1968

Done in the aftermath of the students and workers uprising in Paris in 1968, this fly poster features Crumb's well known character 'Mr Natural'.

MAGAZINE, GANDALF'S GARDEN
ISSUES 1 AND 2, BRITISH, 1968

Gandalf's Garden was a mystical 'Hippy' community that, besides publishing a magazine, also ran a shop and meeting place at World's End in the Chelsea area of London. In the basement was a shrine room were the homeless could 'crash' during the day and 'spiritual' meetings were held every evening with representatives of every spiritual tradition. The magazine, started in 1968, only ran for six issues. Contributors included the poet Christopher Logue, the singer Joan Baez, the DJ John Peel, the comedian and satirist Spike Milligan, and graphic designer Barney Bubbles. Although the designer of issue number 1 is unknown, the designer of number 2 was John Hurford, the other covers were by Muz Murray and Henk t'Jong.

issue one   MAY

fear not—for you are now entering

GANDALF'S GARDEN

issue 2 · 3/-

Big O Posters were sold through *Oz* magazine, many developed from *Oz* covers and artwork. 'Jail the First Stone', a three-dimensional poster, is a comment on the trial of Mick Jagger, along with Keith Richards and the gallery owner Robert Fraser, for drug offences in 1967. The trial occasioned the well known headline in the London *Times*, 'Who Breaks a Butterfly on a Wheel?', a critical comment on the harsh sentence Jagger received.

POSTER, 'EXPLOSION', MARTIN SHARP
BIG O POSTERS, BRITISH, 1967

Created in the 'Summer of Love', this is one of Sharp's most popular posters, in which he successfully captured the power of Jimi Hendrix's music when listened to under the influence of psychedelic drugs.

POSTER, 'BLOWING IN THE MIND/MR TAMBOURINE MAN'
MARTIN SHARP, BIG O POSTERS, BRITISH, 1967

Considered by many to be Sharp's masterpiece, and one of the greatest pieces of Pop graphic art, this expressive portrait of Bob Dylan, in a shimmering mixture of dayglo reds on a gold foil background, personifies the psychedelic experience. It was originally a front cover of *Oz*, no.7, October, 1967.

POSTER, 'DYLAN', MILTON GLASER
AMERICAN, 1967

Milton Glaser was commissioned by Columbia Records to design this poster as an inclusion in the packaging of their 1967 album *Bob Dylan's Greatest Hits*. It is estimated that six million were distributed with this enormously popular record. Glaser, joint founder with Seymour Chawst of New York's Push Pin studio, was America's leading graphic designer in the 1950s and 1960s.

POSTER, 'JUDY GARLAND'
SEYMOUR CHAWST, AMERICAN, 1968

Seymour Chawst, Milton Glaser's partner at the Push Pin Studio, designed this poster for Judy Garland's concert, held at the Philharmonic Hall in New York's Lincoln Centre, on 25th February, 1968. Like Glaser's 'Dylan', it shows the growing influence of psychedelia in mainstream graphic design.

POSTER, 'A IS FOR APPLE', THE FOOL
ANGLO-DUTCH, 1967

The Fool, an Anglo-Dutch design cooperative, were commissioned by the Beatles to design and make the unique pieces of clothing sold in their short-lived Apple boutique, situated in London's Baker Street. They also designed and painted the mural on the boutique's facade, and this promotional poster, a version of the mural, which was also retailed in the store. The poster's design is a tour de force of psychedelic imagery.

POSTER, 'JOHN LENNON'
RICHARD AVEDON, AMERICAN, 1967

This poster of John Lennon is one of the four of the Beatles commissioned in 1967 by Nems, the company owned by Beatles manager Brian Epstein, from the photographer Richard Avedon. These highly expressive posters are heavily solarised colour images, which emanate the psychedelic experience.

JOHN LENNON photographed by Richard Avedon for Look Magazine

POSTER, 'LOVE ME FILMS', HAPSHASH AND THE COLOURED COAT, BRITISH, 1967

In its elegant refinement, this beautiful poster by Hapshash and the Coloured Coat – Michael English and Nigel Waymouth – exemplifies their unique and subtle blend of psychedelic and Art Nouveau imagery. Other than Martin Sharp, Hapshash created some of the most significant Pop graphic design of the 1960s.

PAPERBACK BOOKS, *LOVE, LOVE, LOVE: THE NEW LOVE POETRY*, CORGI BOOKS, BRITAIN, 1967. *IT'S THE WORLD THAT MAKES THE LOVE GO ROUND: POEMS FROM BREAKTHRU*. CORGI BOOKS, BRITAIN, 1968

The covers of these paperbacks of love poetry are again by Hapshash and the Coloured Coat, who as well as poster art, turned their attention to a wide variety of graphic design in the later 1960s.

POSTER, 'MORGAN LE FAYTHFUL'
PETER BLAKE, BRITISH, 1968

Blake was commissioned by the *Daily Telegraph* to design the cover of its weekly magazine for 10th April, 1968, which featured an article, 'The Men behind the Poster Boom'. The cover was also available from the *Telegraph* as a poster for three shillings and sixpence, (17.5 pence). Probably a satirical reference to the City of London's response to the economic disaster of the recent devaluation of the pound in November 1967, the poster features the heroic figure of the singer Marianne Faithfull set against the ruins of the City, which shelter some cheeky Cockneys. Faithfull actually posed for the image, the work of the photographer Michael Cooper, earlier responsible for the photography for the Sgt. Pepper album. The dragon which accompanies her is a 'soft' sculpture by Blake's first wife, the Pop sculptor Jann Haworth, who also contributed to the design of the Sgt. Pepper sleeve.

'BABE RAINBOW', PETER BLAKE
DODO DESIGNS, BRITISH, 1968

Although apparently a poster, this is in fact a screen print on tin, done in emulation of Victorian and Edwardian tinplate advertisements. It was commissioned from the Pop artist Peter Blake by Dodo, London's leading Pop store, who issued it in an edition of ten thousand. Its subject is the fictitious daughter of the 'notorious Dr K. Torture', an earlier fictitious wrestling character devised by Blake.

POSTER, 'MERTON OF THE MOVIES'
ROY LICHTENSTEIN, AMERICAN, 1968

Lichtenstein's poster was created for the Minnesota Theatre Company's 1968 revival of George S. Kaufman's and Marc Connelly's play of 1922, 'Merton of the Movies'. The production was staged at the Tyrone Guthrie Theatre, Minneapolis.

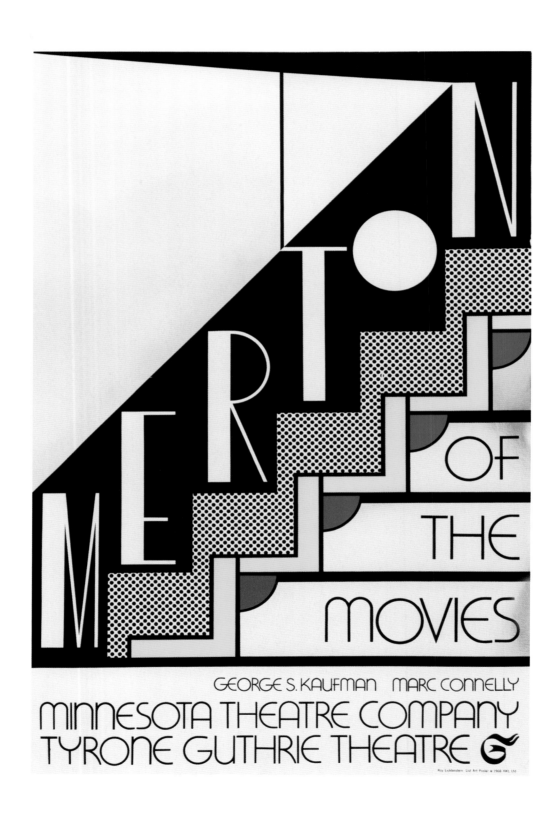

POSTER, 'FOLLIES', DAVID EDWARD BYRD
AMERICAN, 1971

David Edward Byrd is a graphic artist and illustrator who first achieved recognition in the late 60s when he became the sole designer of posters and other graphics for Bill Graham's New York venue, the Fillmore East ballroom in Manhattan's east village. While there he designed memorable posters for concerts by the Grateful Dead, Jimi Hendrix and Jefferson Airplane. He also created posters for the Rolling Stones 1971 world tour, and major musicals such as *Godspell*, *Jesus Christ Superstar*, and this, for *Follies* by Stephen Sondheim. Byrd's work is remarkable in being a highly successful, but uncompromised, crossover of Pop with mainstream commercial graphic design.

POSTER, STANLEY MOUSE AND ALTON KELLEY, GRATEFUL DEAD CONCERT AMERICAN, 1966

Griffin, Mouse and Kelley are three of the five principal graphic artists who created the style of psychedelic West Coast Rock posters used by the various San Francisco music venues in the late 1960s. The other two are Victor Moscoso and Wes Wilson. Of these five, Moscoso is the only formally trained artist and designer, the others, although highly talented are largely self-taught.

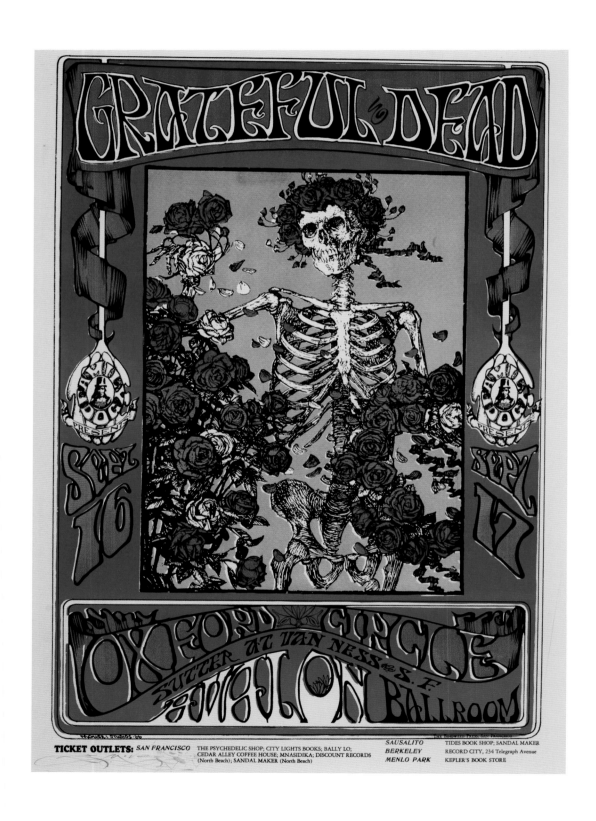

POSTER, RICK GRIFFIN, CONCERT BY JIMI HENDRIX, JOHN MAYALL AND ALBERT KING, AMERICAN, 1968

Rick Griffin's poster for Hendrix and John Mayall features his trademark 'Eyeball' motif, while in Mouse and Kelley's for the Grateful Dead, the influence of fin de siècle art and illustration is apparent.

POSTER FOR A CHAMBERS BROTHERS CONCERT AT THE MATRIX, VICTOR MOSCOSO, NEON ROSE SERIES NO. 12 AMERICAN, 1967

Moscoso considers his poster for the Chambers Brothers concert, Neon Rose series no.12, the most successful and iconic of his images, and indeed it is probably one of the most successful American Pop designs of the 1960s.

POSTER FOR A JEFFERSON AIRPLANE AND QUICKSILVER
MESSENGER SERVICE CONCERT AT THE FILMORE
AUDITORIUM, SAN FRANCISCO, WES WILSON
AMERICAN, 1967

198 UNDERGROUND POSTERS & GRAPHICS 1966–1973

POSTER FOR A BYRDS AND MOBY GRAPE CONCERT AT THE FILMORE AUDITORIUM, WES WILSON AMERICAN, 1967

Considered a pioneer of psychedelic poster art, Wes Wilson created a huge body of posters for the music venues of San Francisco. His achievement was recognised in 1968, when he received a five thousand dollar award from the National Endowment of the Arts for his 'contributions to American art'.

POSTER, 'DYLAN, DON'T LOOK BACK'
ALAN ALDRIDGE, WITH HARRY WILCOX
MOTIF EDITIONS, BRITISH, 1967

Alan Aldridge, who describes himself as a 'Graphic Entertainer', was probably the most successful British graphic designer of the 1960s. By 1965 he was art director of Penguin Books at the age of twenty two, and subsequently illustrated *The Beatles Illustrated Lyrics*, and designed the poster for Andy Warhol's film, *Chelsea Girls*. He designed this poster in 1967 for D.A. Pennebaker's film of Dylan's 1965 British tour, *Don't Look Back*.

POSTER FOR *THE GREAT AMERICAN DISASTER*, ALAN ALDRIDGE, BRITISH, 1970

Aldridge designed this promotional poster for The Great American Disaster, the first authentic American burger joint in Britain, with 'all the fixin's', like sweetcorn relish, available for the discerning diner. It opened in London's Fulham Road in April 1970.

THE FUN PALACE
1969–1973

A PAIR OF SHORTS BY SYLVIA AYTON IN ZANDRA RHODES' 'LIPSTICK' FABRIC, BRITISH, c1967.
A 'KIPPER' TIE BY FOALE AND TUFFIN USING ZANDRA RHODES' 'LIGHT BULB' FABRIC, c1966

Rhodes' remarkable series of 'Lipstick' and 'Light Bulb' prints, some of the first British Pop textiles, date from the early period of her work as a professional designer in the mid-1960s. The shorts were designed by the fashion designer Sylvia Ayton, who, like Rhodes, was then a recent graduate from the Royal College of Art. At that time Ayton and Rhodes worked together to sell their designs wholesale, but shortly after, with the backing of, amongst others, the actress Vanessa Redgrave, they opened the Fulham Road Clothes Shop. Their model then was Rhodes' friend, the broadcaster, writer and journalist, Janet Street-Porter, to whom these shorts once belonged. After graduating, Rhodes had difficulty finding a ready market for her fashion textiles. Her first success came when two other graduates from the Royal College, the fashion designers Marion Foale and Sally Tuffin, began to use them, such as the 'Light Bulb' textile used for this 'kipper' tie.

'AMERICAN FOOTBALL' SCREEN-PRINTED TEXTILE
JANE WEALLEANS FOR MR FREEDOM, BRITISH, 1970

This cotton crepe border print, intended for dresses and blouses, was designed by the textile designer Jane Wealleans, the wife of Jon Wealleans, then principal interior designer for Mr Freedom. It had a very limited production of probably less than thirty metres, and Tommy Roberts recalls only a handful of blouses and one dress being made from it. Wealleans and her partner Sue Saunders subsequently set up OK Textiles, working under the slogan 'If It Runs We Chase It.'

AMERICAN BASEBALL SUIT, DIANA CRAWSHAW FOR MR FREEDOM, BRITISH, 1970. THE MR FREEDOM LABEL GEORGE HARDIE, BRITISH, 1969

This baseball ensemble, by the fashion designer Diana Crawshaw, a graduate of the Royal College of Art, is one of the most celebrated designs created for Mr Freedom. Crawshaw was one of a number of designers, nearly all graduates of the Royal College, from whom Roberts commissioned designs. Amongst them were the graphic designer Tony Wright, the fashion designers John and Molly Dove, Dinah Adams and Jim O'Connor, and the textile designer Chris Snow. The Mr Freedom label was designed by another Royal College graduate, the graphic designer George Hardie. He created the overall graphic identity of Mr Freedom, designing the letterheads, the menus, and even the labels for the wine bottles used in the 'Mr Feed'Em' restaurant, housed in the basement of the Mr Freedom boutique in Kensington High Street.

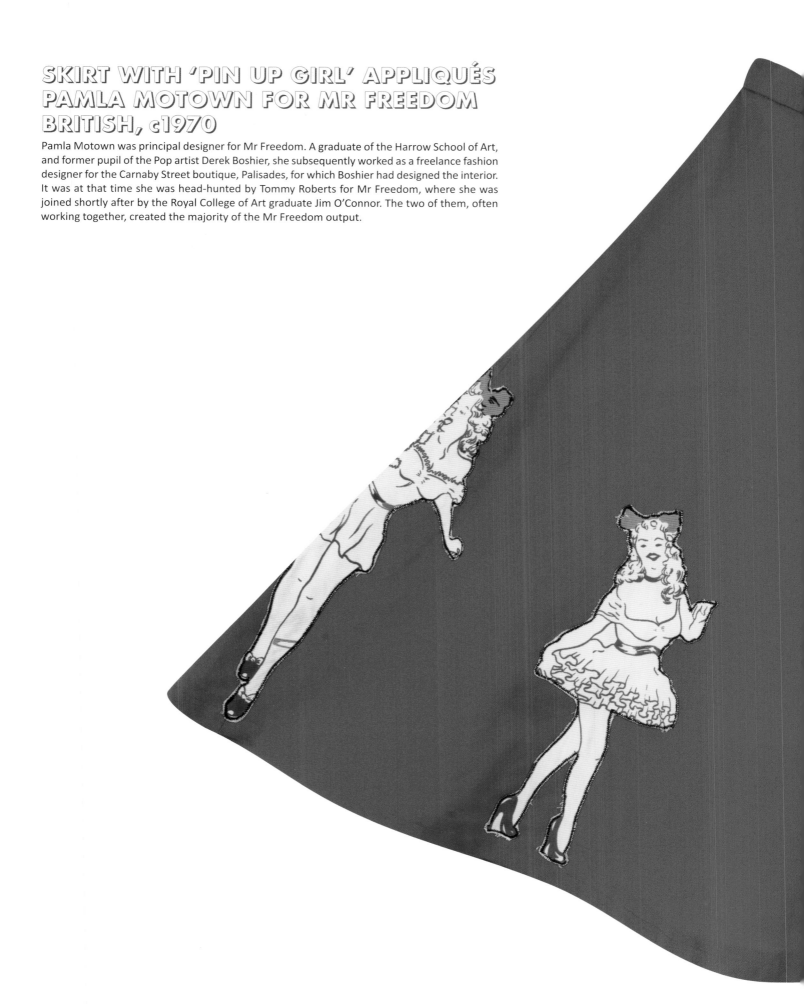

SKIRT WITH 'PIN UP GIRL' APPLIQUÉS
PAMLA MOTOWN FOR MR FREEDOM
BRITISH, c1970

Pamla Motown was principal designer for Mr Freedom. A graduate of the Harrow School of Art, and former pupil of the Pop artist Derek Boshier, she subsequently worked as a freelance fashion designer for the Carnaby Street boutique, Palisades, for which Boshier had designed the interior. It was at that time she was head-hunted by Tommy Roberts for Mr Freedom, where she was joined shortly after by the Royal College of Art graduate Jim O'Connor. The two of them, often working together, created the majority of the Mr Freedom output.

'OODLES OF POODLES' JACKET, BRENT SHERWOOD FOR MR FREEDOM, BRITISH c1970

Many of Mr Freedom's clients were leading Pop musicians and celebrities, amongst whom were Mick Jagger, Olivia Newton John and Marc Bolan. One of the boutique's biggest fans was Elton John, who wore an 'Oodles of Poodles' jacket when he and Marc Bolan appeared together on Top of the Pops in 1971 playing 'Get It On'.

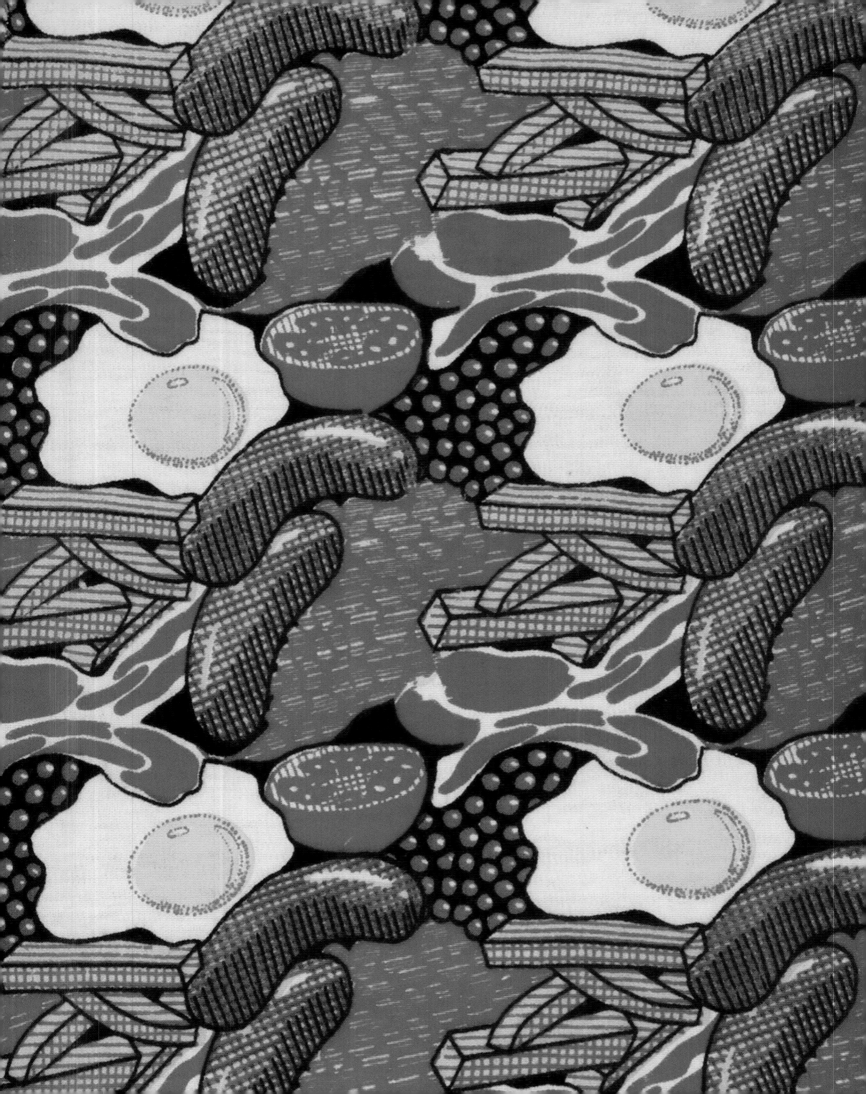

'FRY UP' THEMED LONG-SLEEVED T-SHIRT, PAMLA MOTOWN FOR MARSHALL LESTER, BRITISH, 1972

Pamla Motown and Jim O'Connor left Mr Freedom at the end of 1971 to set up their own design studio, Two Generators. They worked on a freelance basis for people in the fashion trade, like the designer Jeff Banks, and the manufacturer Marshall Lester, whose principal product was T-Shirts. This long sleeved 'Fry Up' T-shirt, manufactured by Marshall Lester, dates from this time, and was sold by Mr Freedom, together with another by Motown with a design of 'Liquorice Allsorts' confectionery.

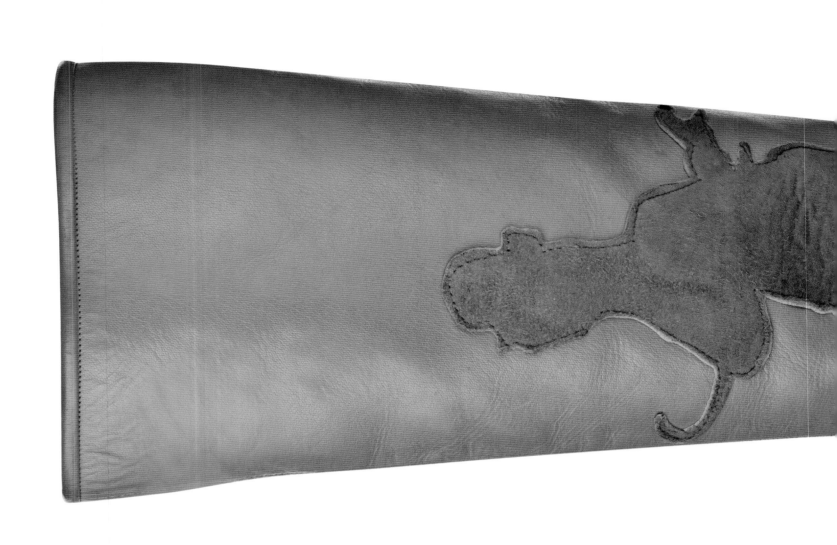

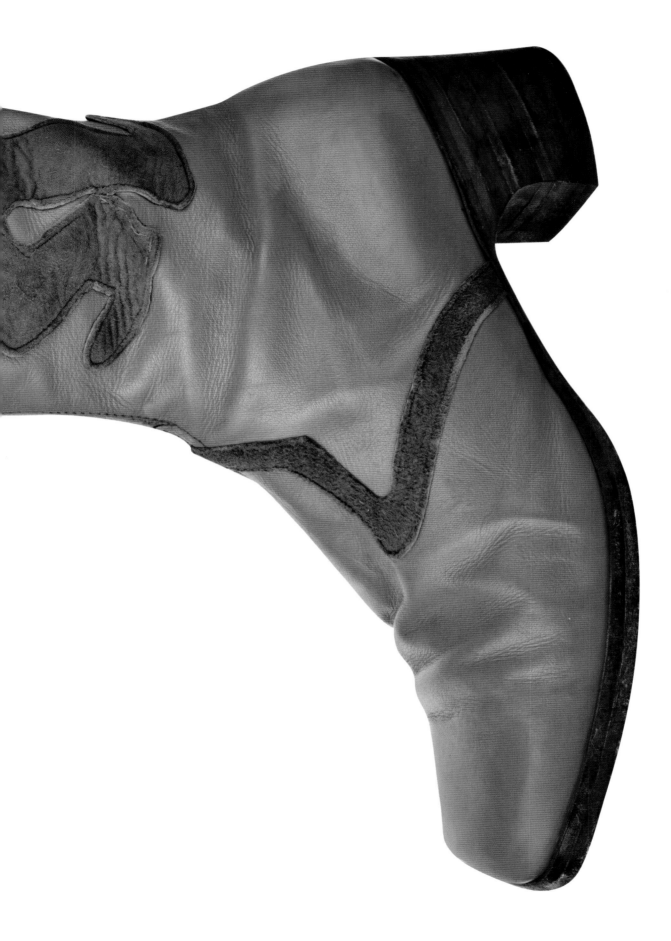

PAIR OF BOOTS DECORATED WITH SUEDE APPLIQUÉS OF CHARLIE CHAPLIN, MR FREEDOM, BRITISH, c1970

Hollywood film stars were a favourite theme of Mr Freedom designers, cartoon characters were another. Mr Freedom was the first fashion company awarded a licence by the Disney Corporation, which allowed them to use Walt Disney's characters for the decoration of clothing, such as the tops appliquéd with a satin Mickey Mouse, or dresses printed with images of Pinnochio.

PAIR OF PEARLISED LEATHER, SUEDE AND SNAKESKIN WEDGE-HEELED SHOES AND A COMPANION LEATHER BELT WITH PAINTED DECORATION AND APPLIQUÉD EMBROIDERY, MR FREEDOM, BRITISH, c1970

This unique pair of wedge-heeled shoes and belt were a special order. Mr Freedom was well known for carrying out such commissions, for instance, outfits were specially-created by the Mr Freedom designers for Elton John, one of the Boutique's regular clients.

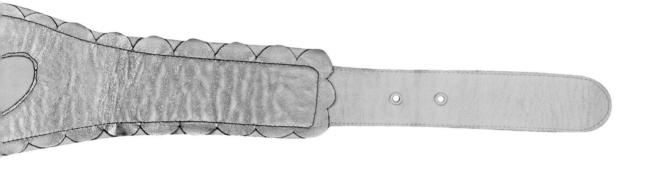

PAIR OF MEN'S PLATFORM BOOTS, BRITISH, c1971
PAIR OF WOMEN'S PLATFORM MULES
SACHA LONDON, BRITISH, c1971

Extravagantly decorated and colourful, platform shoes were extremely fashionable for both men and women in the late 1960s and early 1970s. Both of these pairs have platform soles combined with high heels. They are handmade, the soles and heels of the mules are of carved wood, and the heels of the boots of 'stacked' leather. The boots are identical to a pair owned by Elton John, but in a different combination of coloured leathers.

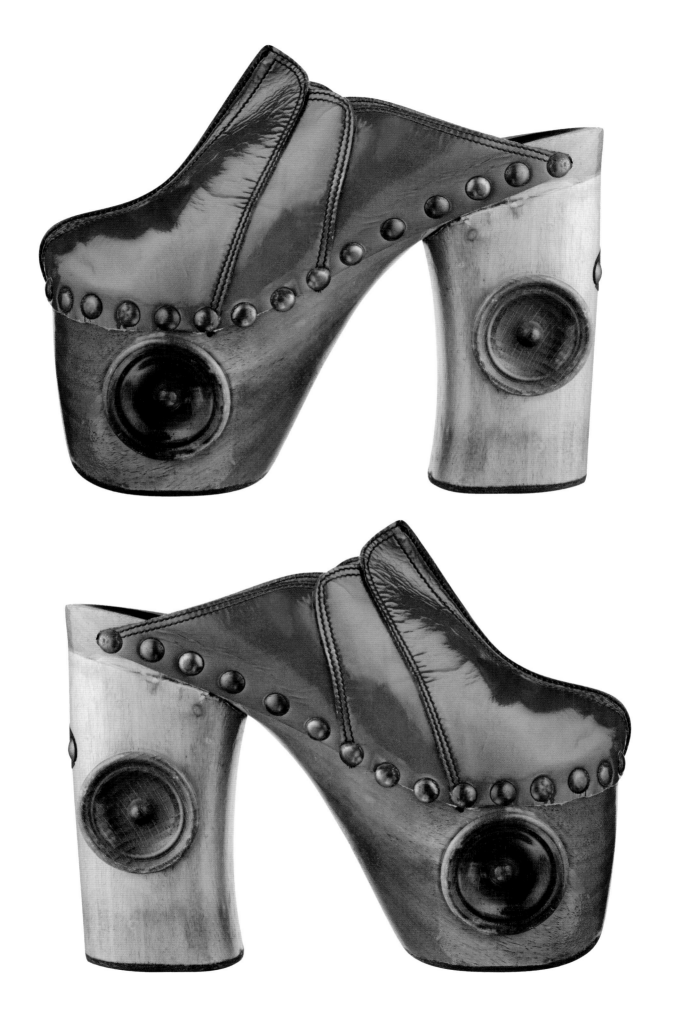

WOMAN'S SHORT JACKET BY KITSCH, MADE IN 'SPACE WALK', A SCREEN-PRINTED COTTON TEXTILE DESIGNED BY SUE THATCHER FOR WARNER AND SON LTD, 1969

'Space Walk' was produced to commemorate the American moon landing in 1969, and the bravery and adventurous spirit of the astronauts who made it possible. The designer, Sue Thatcher, worked in the Warner and Sons London studio between 1967 and 1971.

222 THE FUN PALACE 1969–1973

JVC 'VIDEOSPHERE', JAPAN, 1970

The Japanese electronics company JVC introduced their 'Videosphere' portable television in 1970. Shaped like an astronaut's helmet, its design was influenced by the 1969 moon landing and the popularity of Stanley Kubrick's 1968 film *2001, A Space Odyssey*. Available in white, black, red or orange, the 'Videosphere' proved extremely successful.

THE FABRIC OF POP

A TRAVELLING EXHIBITION ARRANGED BY THE CIRCULATION DEPARTMENT OF THE VICTORIA & ALBERT MUSEUM

SHIRT MADE FROM LLOYD JOHNSON'S SCREEN-PRINTED COTTON TEXTILE 'SOUP CAN', JOHNSON AND JOHNSON BRITISH, 1973

In the early 1970s Lloyd Johnson created clothing using Pop textiles he'd designed, such as 'Soup Can', which he marketed under his own label Johnson and Johnson. He also used 'Fred', his textile based on a film still of Fred Astaire in the movie 'Top Hat', for jackets, Astaire was subsequently photographed wearing one. 'Legs', a printed textile by Jane Wealleans of OK Textiles, was also used by Johnson for shirts and jackets, one of which was owned by Elton John. Pop textiles designed both by Johnson and Wealleans, were exhibited in the Victoria & Albert Museum's 1974 travelling exhibition 'The Fabric of Pop'.

225

**OPPOSITE: MARY QUANT 'LIPSTICK' TRANSISTOR RADIO AND PACKAGING, BRITISH, LATE 1960S
BELOW: MARY QUANT LIPSTICK, BRITISH, LATE 1960**

This radio and packaging, a giant version of the Mary Quant lipstick, is in the spirit of the surreal Pop sculptures by the Swedish American Pop artist Claes Oldenburg, who created greatly-enlarged replicas of everyday objects which emphasised their fetishistic nature.

227

OPPOSITE: THREE INFLATABLE CUSHIONS FROM A SERIES DESIGNED BY PETER MAX AMERICAN c1968. ABOVE: THREE SILK-SCREEN PRINTED COTTON CUSHIONS DESIGNED BY SIMON EVA FOR GEAR OF CARNABY STREET, BRITISH, c1968

As high Pop interiors became increasingly informal, traditional forms of seating were replaced with inexpensive bean bags and gigantic cushions placed at floor level. Smaller cushions, such as these, were either scattered amongst them, or in heaps on divans or mattresses, which served both for seating and sleeping. While Peter Max's inflatable cushions are decorated with well known images from his distinctive oeuvre, Simon Eva's are screen-printed with images of Hollywood stars, such as Clint Eastwood or Charlie Chaplin, in a Warholian-influenced 'fun' style.

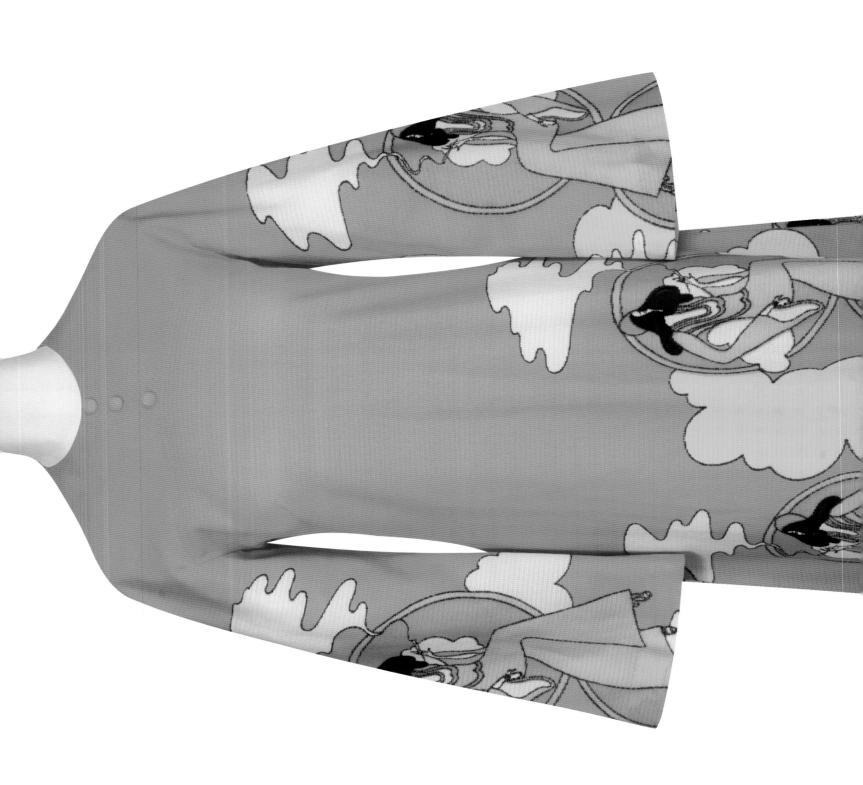

CRUISE DRESS BY SPORTAVILLE, BRITISH, c1969

The British fashion company Sportaville produced a considerable amount of Pop designed clothing in the late 1960s. This maxi dress, unashamedly realised in a lightweight man-made non-iron 'Wonder' material, was guaranteed to remain crease- free while travelling. Its vividly coloured large-scale pattern of Art Deco inspired 'smoking' women refers to both the work of Peter Max and, even more so, to the palette and style of Heinz Edelmann's design for the Beatles animated film, *The Yellow Submarine.*

LOW LACQUERED TABLE, BIBA, BRITISH, c1974

One of the success stories of British Pop design in the 1960s was that of Barbara Hulanicki's famed boutique Biba. Originally a mail order fashion business, it became a boutique which progressed though the 60s to ever bigger locations until its final move, in 1974, to the seven storey building of the former Derry & Toms department store on London's Kensington High Street. The Big Biba store was on a vast scale, with one floor dedicated to the home; selling furniture, soft furnishings and wallpaper. The store was a late manifestation of 'Fun' Pop, its fittings strongly influenced by the work of the American Pop sculptor Claes Oldenburg. For instance, the record department was dominated by a giant record player, while the food hall's display units were oversized tin cans, one labelled 'Warhol's Condensed Soup'. Unfortunately, mainly due to its all-encompassing conception, Big Biba overreached itself and closed after a very short time in 1975. The image which decorates the top of this lacquered table is the epitome of the idealized Biba girl.

'MICKEY MOUSE' OCCASIONAL TABLE, BRITISH, c1969

This table is a rare piece of late 60s Pop furniture, mainly designed for and retailed by small London boutiques such as Luckies or Mr Freedom. Furniture of this type was either specially made to order, or in very limited productions of two or three examples.

'THEM'
THE ART BRIGADE
PROTO POST-
MODERNISM
1970–1976

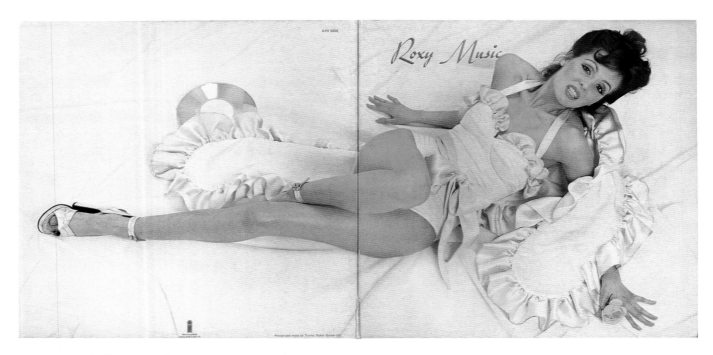

LP RECORD SLEEVE, *ROXY MUSIC*, BY ROXY MUSIC, THE BAND'S DEBUT ALBUM, BRITISH, 1972. HIGH HEELED PEEP-TOE SHOE TERRY DE HAVILLAND, BRITISH, c1971

Roxy Music first album is a summation of the interrelatedness of Pop musicians, designers and artists, and a realisation of the Pop artist Richard Hamilton's teaching. For Bryan Ferry, Roxy Music – its style, music, fashions and graphic design – was the actualisation of the creative and cultural parity he saw, like Hamilton, between art and Pop. The sleeve's glamorous image of the model Kari-Ann Muller, a knowing pastiche of a 1940s pin-up girl, à la Rita Hayworth, was the cooperative achievement of a remarkable constellation of talent. The concept for the sleeve was Ferry's, while the fashion designer Anthony Price, responsible for the sleeve's overall styling, created Kari-Ann's costume, and the avant-garde hairdresser Keith Wainwright at Smile, her hair. The album's art director Nick de Ville, like Ferry, a former student of Richard Hamilton, was also his studio assistant. The shoe is one of a pair by the leading London shoemaker and designer, Terry de Havilland, who described himself as a 'Rock 'n' Roll cobbler'. He set up his first boutique, Cobblers to The World, in 1972.

Roxy's second album, *For Your Pleasure*, took the artistic collaboration of Pop designers and artists even further. The album's gatefold sleeve opens to reveal Roxy's band members, each in a costume by a different designer. Brian Eno wears the now iconic costume created for him by his then partner, the Pop artist and ceramist Carol McNicoll, Antony Price designed Bryan Ferry's outfit, and Andy Mackay's was the work of the former Mr Freedom designers, Pamla Motown and Jim O'Connor. Wendy Dagworthy, the present head of fashion at the Royal College of Art, designed Phil Manzanera's outfit, and hair styling was again by Keith Wainwright at Smile.

FOR YOUR PLEASURE...
The second Roxy Music Album

Photography – Karl Stoecker
Art direction – Nicholas de Ville
Artwork – C.C.S.
Amanda's clothes, hair and
make-up – Anthony Price
Roxy hair – Smile
Crew – Jennings and Hart
℗ Island Records 1973

SIDE ONE
Do the Strand
Beauty Queen
Strictly Confidential
Editions of You
In every Dream Home a Heartache

ANDREW MACKAY

PAUL THOMPSON

DE TWO
e Bogus Man
ey Lagoons
your Pleasure

rds and Music by Bryan Ferry

Bryan Ferry – Voice and Keyboards
Andrew Mackay – Oboe and Saxophone
Eno – Synthesizer and Tapes
Paul Thompson – 'Drums
Phil Manzanera – Guitar
Guest artiste : John Porter – Bass

Recorded at AIR Studios
London, February 1973
Engineers: John Middleton and John Punter
Produced by Chris Thomas and Roxy Music
for E. G. Records
Special thanks to John Anthony
All songs arranged by Roxy Music
All songs published by E. G. Music Ltd © 1973

island records ltd
bassing street london w1

CERAMIC QUILTED 'BUTTON FLOWER' DISH, CAROL MCNICOLL, BRITISH, 1972

This dish is part of a dinner service Zandra Rhodes commissioned from Carol McNicoll in 1972, who included it in her degree show that year. McNicoll made the service by ingeniously joining cast ceramic shapes to create dishes, bowls and plates in the form of quilts, cushions and pillows, which she decorated with Rhodes's Pop pattern, 'Button Flower'. McNicoll was one of the young ceramists whose work was considered part of the revolutionary 'New Ceramics' of the 1970s. ('Button Flower' dish courtesy Zandra Rhodes)

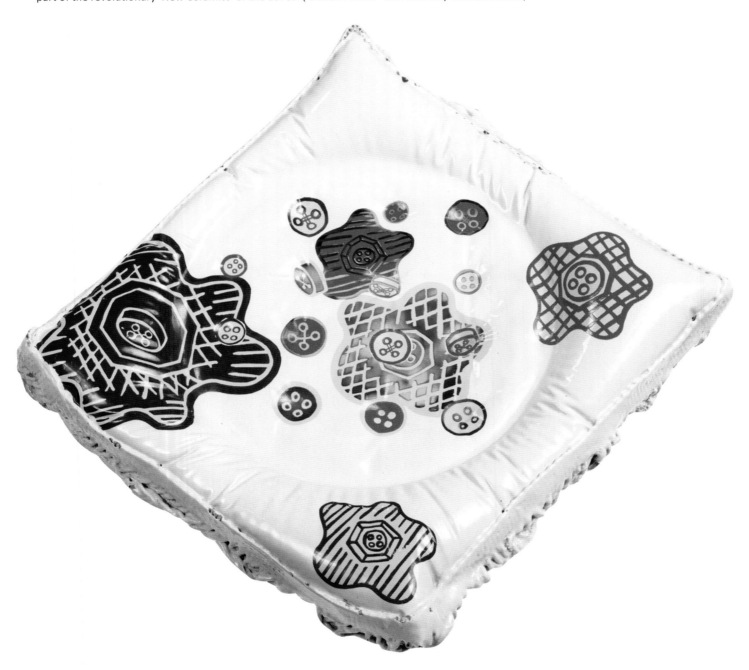

'DINOSAUR' COAT AND HAT, ZANDRA RHODES, BRITISH 1971. PHOTOGRAPHER, DAVID BAILEY, BRITISH, 1971 MODEL, PENELOPE TREE, AMERICAN

Amongst the most extreme of Rhodes' fashion designs, her 'Dinosaur' clothes are certainly the most sculptural. The example worn here by the American model Penelope Tree, and photographed by David Bailey, consists of a coat, knee-length culottes and 'Halo' hat, printed and appliquéd with the 'Button Flower' pattern. (Photograph of Penelope Tree courtesy of David Bailey)

240 'THEM' 1970–1976

PORTRAIT OF ZANDRA RHODES AND CHELITA SECUNDA
DUGGIE FIELDS, BRITISH, 1972

Duggie Fields was, more or less, painter by appointment to 'Them'. This portrait of Zandra Rhodes and her friend the fashion journalist and stylist Chelita Secunda, is an example of Field's unsettling and subversive version of Pop art, in which he plays with disembodied 1950s amorphous kitsch forms and truncated images to create work suffused with a vaguely sinister, erotic undercurrent. In the portrait Rhodes wears a 'Dinosaur' suit like that worn by Penelope Tree. (Portrait courtesy Zandra Rhodes)

INTERIOR, DUGGIE FIELDS, BRITISH, 1974

Possibly more than anyone, Duggie Fields is the living embodiment of Richard Hamilton's concept of Pop; for him life and art are one. The redesigning and redecorating of the interior of his flat in the Earls Court area of London, his home since 1968, has become an intrinsic part of his art. In this photograph he wears a shirt made from one of his own textiles, which he has also used for the interior's soft furnishings. His shoes are decorated with the same pattern. (Photograph courtesy Duggie Fields)

244 'THEM' 1970–1976

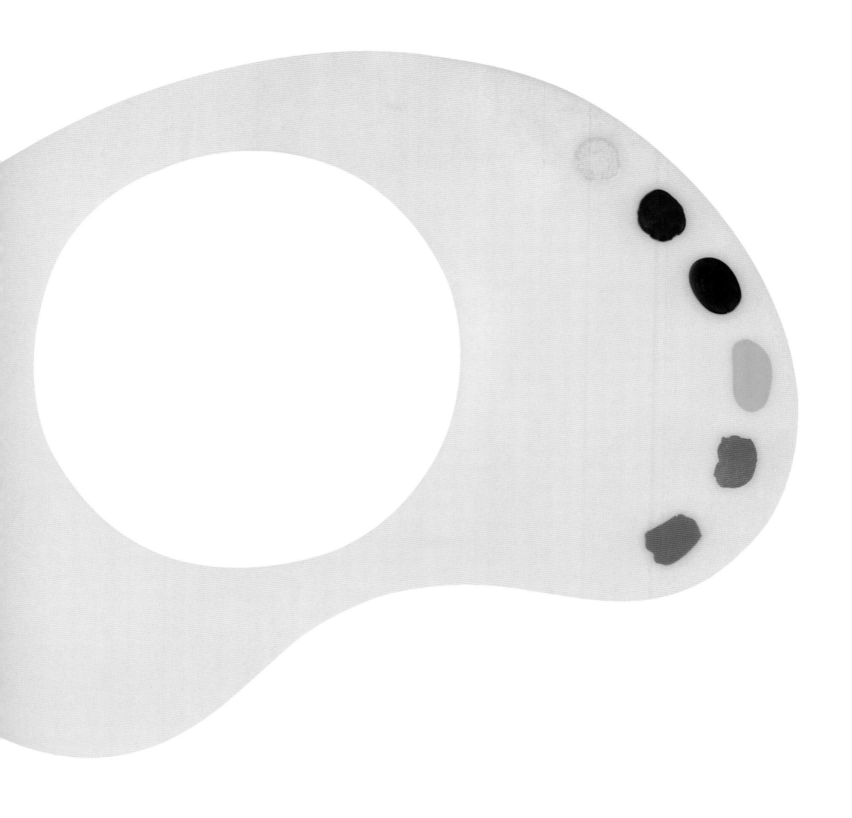

PALETTE COLLAR AND BANGLE, BRITISH, c1972

`The artist's palette, so popular in 1950s kitsch design, became a *leitmotiv* of 1970s and early 1980s design. Both Duggie Fields and his friend Rae Spencer-Cullen frequently referenced it in their work, and it was used a little earlier for a 'Painter's Smock' garment for the Mr Freedom boutique.

DRESS AND SKIRT, MISS MOUSE, BRITISH, EARLY 1970S

The fashion and textile designer Rae Spencer-Cullen worked under the labels, 'Miss Mouse' and 'Miss Mouse at Squeakers'. Her designs were witty 'camp' pastiches of popular fashions and patterns from the 1950s, which anticipated certain aspects of 1980s fashion and Post Modernism. She was a close friend of Duggie Fields who, like her, also referenced 1940s and 1950s kitsch patterns in his work. Very much a 'Them' designer, she took part in Derek Jarman's 1976 film, *Sebastiane*, and in 1978 created the host/hostess gown for Andrew Logan's 'Alternative Miss World' competition.

247

In 1972, the sculptor and jeweller Andrew Logan inaugurated the ultimate 'Them' event, the 'Alternative Miss World' competition. Open to all, it continues still, an ironic non-competitive competition, with no restrictions on contestants, who can be whoever or whatever they wish. The event is a fun celebration of ambiguity which challenges traditional perceptions of sexuality, beauty and style.
(Photographs of Andrew Logan and Derek Jarman, courtesy Andrew Logan)

THE FRONT AND BACK OF THE SLEEVE OF LOU REED'S LP, *TRANSFORMER*, ANGLO-AMERICAN, 1972

Styled by Antony Price, who also designed the costumes worn by the models, Gala Mitchell and Ernie Thormahlen, the sleeve of *Transformer* exudes an ambience of camp ambidexterity and sexual ambiguity. When first released the album's imagery was the cause of some confusion, many believing Gala Mitchell and Thormahlen were either one and the same, or even Lou Reed, 'transformed' in an act of high transvestism. Commenting on his role in general, Price observed, 'I'm not a fashion designer... I'm in the theatrical business.'

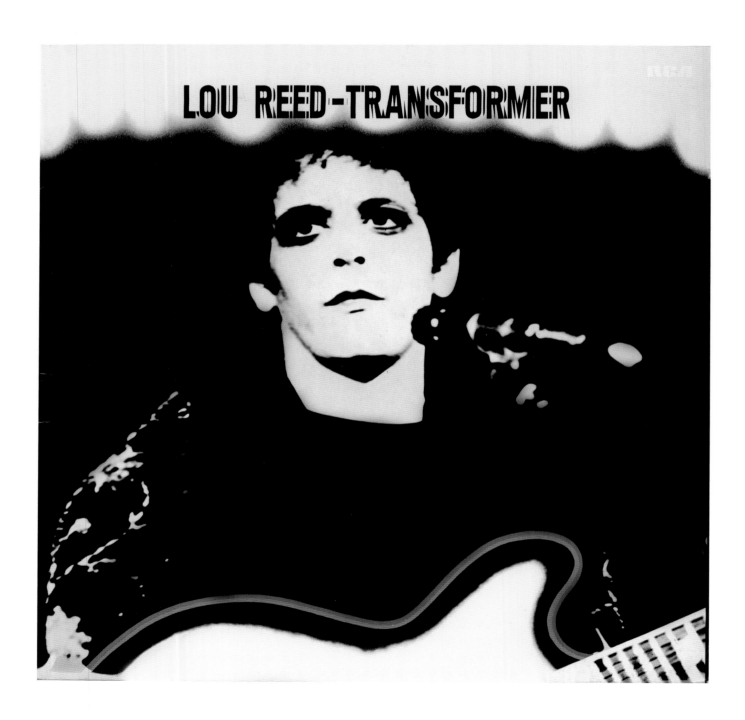

LOU REED-TRANSFORMER

SIDE 1	SIDE 2
Vicious	Make Up
Andy's Chest	Satellite of Love
Perfect Day	Wagon Wheel
Hangin' 'Round	New York Telephone Conversation
Walk on the Wild Side	I'm So Free
	Goodnight Ladies

"Stereo records give full stereo reproduction when played on a stereo record player. They can be played on most modern mono record players fitted with a lightweight tone arm and pick-up head and the sound reproduction will be monaural. If you have doubts and wish to avoid damaging your equipment or records, consult your dealer."

All songs written by Lou Reed
Produced by David Bowie and Mick Ronson
Song Arrangements: Lou Reed, David Bowie and Mick Ronson
String and Bass Arrangements: Mick Ronson

David Bowie, Mick Ronson and The Thunder Thighs, *vocal backings*
Lou Reed, Mick Ronson, *guitars*
Klaus Voorman, Herbie Flowers, *bass guitars*
Herbie Flowers, *string bass*
John Halzey*, Barry Desouza, Ritchie Dharma, *drums*
"Goodnight Ladies" arranged and played by
Herbie Flowers and some of his friends
Herbie Flowers, *tuba*
Ronnie Ross, *baritone sax*
Mick Ronson, *piano and recorders*
*By courtesy of Island Records Ltd

Mixed by Ken Scott, Mike Stone, Lou Reed, David Bowie and Mick Ronson
at Trident Studios, London, England
Tape mastering by Arun Chakranerty
Lou Reed managed exclusively by Fred Heller Management Enterprises
40 Cedar Street, Dobbs Ferry, New York 10522   (914) 693-6200
Art Direction and Design: Ernst Thormahlen
Color Photographs: Karl Stoeker
Black and White Photographs: Mick Rock

251

The darkly glittering 'Mephistophelian' sleeve of *For Your Pleasure* evokes an ambiguous world of sinister excess. The mysterious model, singer and writer Amanda Lear, who teeters seductively across the sleeve, led by a snarling black panther, was, in actuality, the epitome of ambiguity, with nothing of her age, origins, and gender certain or confirmed. Beloved in turn by the Rolling Stone Brian Jones, Bryan Ferry, and David Bowie, she was also muse and mistress of the painter Salvador Dali. She is completely the result of artifice, a Pop artefact, described in the Sunday Times magazine in 1985 as '… a dream come true by her unique will.' As with the first Roxy album, the concept for the sleeve again came from Bryan Ferry, the art direction was by Nick de Ville, the styling and Lear's costume by Antony Price and her hair by Keith at Smile.

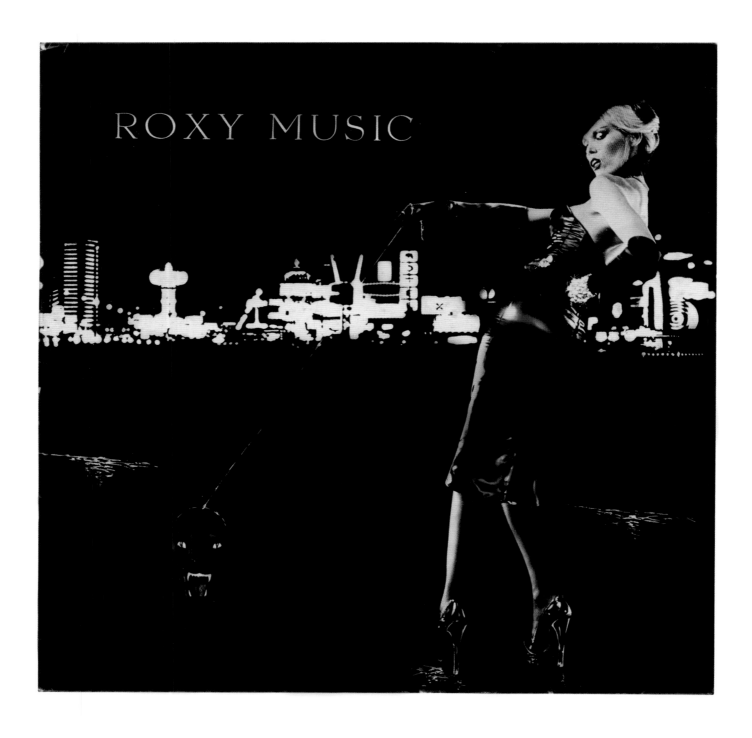

PHOTOGRAPH OF BRYAN FERRY TAKEN FROM THE SLEEVE OF ROXY MUSIC'S FIRST ALBUM, BRITISH, 1972

A pastiche of the carefully constructed images of Pop stars in 1950s fanzines, this cliched image of Ferry knowingly refers to the art directed existence of the Pop star. It was said at the time, that Ferry should hang in London's Tate gallery.

Bryan Ferry

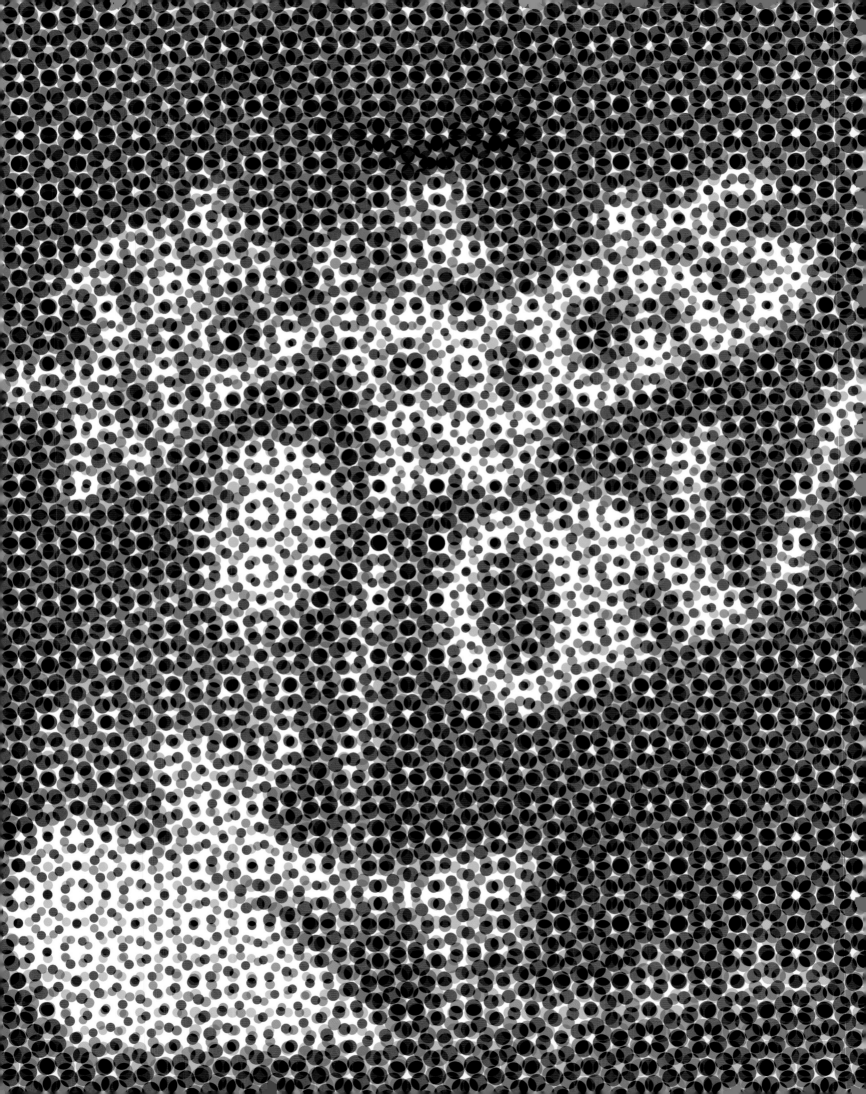

PUNK

RECORD SLEEVE OF THE RAMONES' FIRST LP, AMERICAN, 1976

Generally acknowledged the first true Punk band, the founding of the Ramones in 1974 spearheaded the burgeoning New York Punk movement. Their first album, released in February 1976, was hailed a critical success by the influential magazine *Punk;* the sleeve's now iconic cover photograph was taken by Roberta Bayley, a photographer for the magazine. The band's outfits caused a stir, which, other than the length of their hair, were not Hippy, but something entirely new to the then-flamboyant Rock and Pop scene. A recycling of the basic uniform of 1950s teenage rebels, the band's scruffy jeans, T-shirts and leather jackets soon became essential kit for wannabe punks.

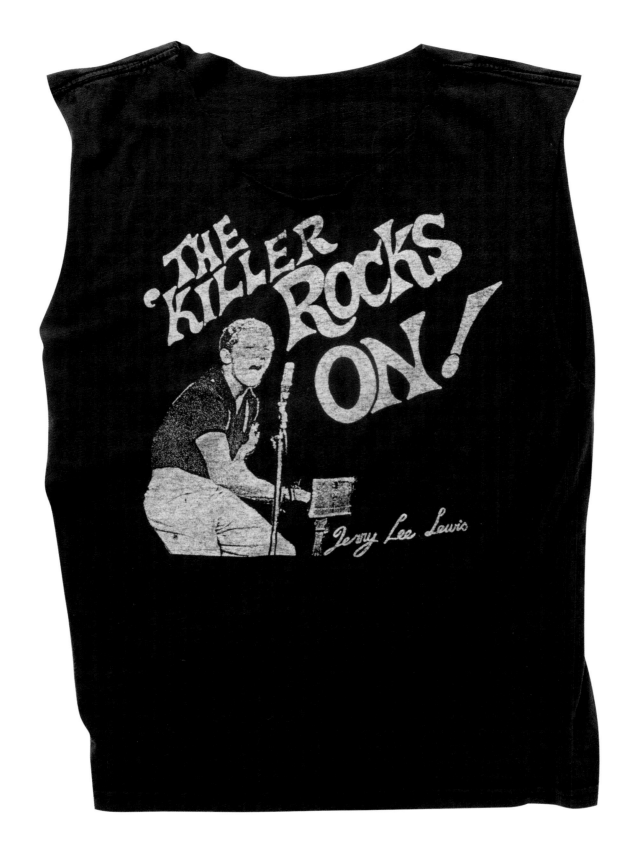

T-SHIRT, 'THE KILLER ROCKS ON', VIVIENNE WESTWOOD AND MALCOLM MCLAREN, BRITISH, 1972

McLaren and Westwood set up their first shop, Let it Rock, in 1971, for which they produced a series of T-shirts, 'People of Rock', including this example, screen-printed with an image of Jerry Lee Lewis. Relatively inexpensive, they remained available throughout the shop's subsequent incarnations in the 1970s, the T-shirt being the one item most youngsters could easily afford.

A PAIR OF 'BONDAGE' BOOTS, VIVIENNE WESTWOOD FOR SEX, BRITISH, c1975

These boots were designed by Westwood for Sex, the third incarnation of her and McLaren's King's Road shop. Its previous identity, Too Fast to Live, Too Young to Die, sold Westwood-designed versions of Biker gear and leathers, which, when the shop transformed into Sex, mutated into sado-masochistic inspired Bondage clothing, that later formed the basis of Punk fashion.

KNITTED MOHAIR AND STRING SWEATER
VIVIENNE WESTWOOD FOR SEX, BRITISH, c1975

Westwood had championed the revival of the mohair sweater since the early days of her first shop, Let It Rock. By the time of Sex, she was creating revolutionary asymmetrical designs, achieved by combining randomly coloured mohair wools with string, this complex sweater being an early example. She continued to produce 'deconstructed' mohair and string sweaters throughout the later Sex and Seditionaries period.

This Bondage shirt is probably the most memorable item of Westwood's Punk fashion designs. Made from an extremely flimsy type of cheesecloth fabric, the shirt was intended to quickly self-destruct, something McLaren emphasised when later confronted with not-inconsiderable quantities of what purported to be immaculate survivors. Jamie Reid's iconic graphic of a disintegrating Union Jack, held together with safety pins and bulldog clips, which explodes across the shirt's front, mirrors those on Pop clothes from the mid-1960s, which also satirized the somewhat threadbare pretentions to international power and dominance of the British establishment. Under the Anarchy symbol, the Seditionaries label ironically lists some of the outsider groups Punks identified with.

for
soldiers
prosti-
tutes
dykes +
punks

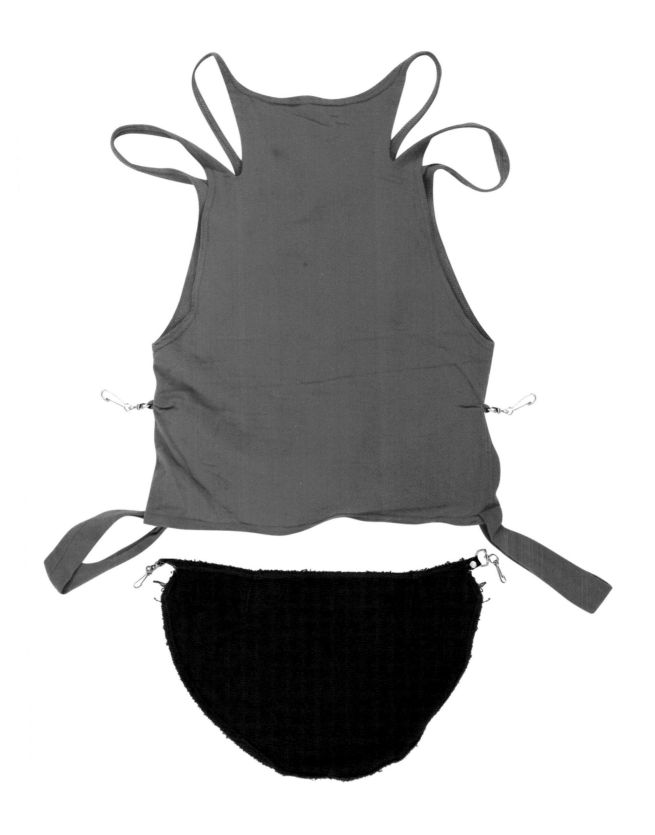

BONDAGE VEST WITH 'BUM FLAP', VIVIENNE WESTWOOD FOR SEDITIONARIES, c1976

Like most of Westwood's designs for Seditionaries, this Bondage vest makes reference to sado-masochistic fetishism. The 'bum flap'- derived from a piece of industrial clothing worn to protect the rear of workmen's pants — was often superfluously added to Punk outfits as a purely decorative detail.

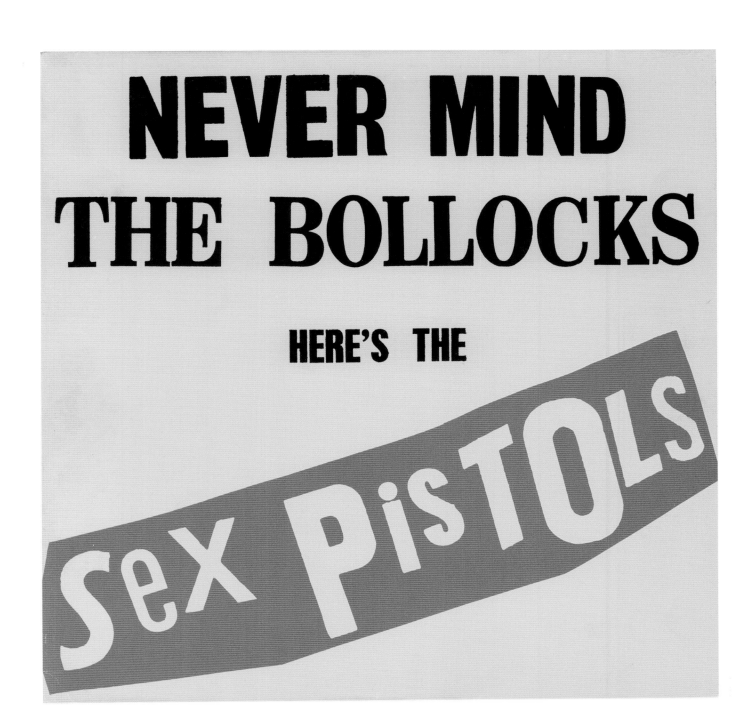

LP RECORD SLEEVE, *NEVER MIND THE BOLLOCKS HERE'S THE SEX PISTOLS*, JAMIE REID, BRITISH, 1977

Like so much else in their brief but momentous career, the Sex Pistols recording history was short, sharp and not too sweet. It resulted in this, their only studio album, released on October 27th 1977, and a handful of singles with Johnny Rotten as singer. Rotten left the band in January 1978, amongst the singles he made with them were the iconic 'Anarchy in the UK' and the notorious 'God Save the Queen'. The design for the LP's sleeve was the work of the graphic designer and anarchist Jamie Reid, a fellow art student and friend of Malcolm McLaren from Croydon School of Art. The release of the album initiated a replay of the *Oz* trial when, following its display in the window of Virgin Records' Nottingham store, the company was taken to court charged with 'displaying indecent printed matter'. However, following an intervention by the lawyer and playwright John Mortimer, who had previously defended the *Oz* editors, the case was thrown out.

APPENDICES

Aldridge Alan, *The Man with Kaleidoscope Eyes: The Art of Alan Aldridge*, Abrams Books, New York, 2009.

Bailey David, Harrison Michael, *David Bailey: Archive One 1957-1969*, Thames and Hudson, London, 1999.

Barnes Richard, *Mods*, Plexus edition, London, 1991.

Barrett Cyril, *An Introduction to Optical Art*, A StudioVista/Dutton Pictureback, London, 1971.

Beaumont Mary Rose, *Duggie Fields: Paintings 1982-1987*, Albermarle Gallery, London, 1987.

Blackman Cally, *One Hundred Years of Menswear*, Laurence King Publishing, London 2009.

Boyd Joe, *White Bicycles: Making Music in the 1960s*, Serpent's Tail, London, 2006.

Bracewell Michael, *Re-Make/Re-Model: Art, Pop, Fashion and the Making of Roxy Music 1952-1972*, Faber and Faber, London, 2007.

Brockris Victor, *Warhol*, DaCapo Press, Cambridge Massachusetts, 1989.

Carrington Noel, Hutton Clarke, *Popular Art in Britain*, Penguin, London 1945.

Colegrave Stephen, Sullivan Chris, *Punk: A Life Apart*, Cassell & Co, London, 2001.

Collins Michael, Papadakis Andreas, *Post-Modern Design*, Academy Editions, London, 1989.

Dean Roger, with Dominy Hamilton, Carla Capallo and Donald Lehmkuhl, *Views*, Dragon's Dream Ltd, Brighton and Paris, 1975.

English Michael with a foreword by Penny Sparke, *3D Eye: The Posters, Prints and Paintings of Michael English*, Paper Tiger a Dragon's World imprint, Limpsfield, 1979.

Fogg Marnie, *Boutique: a '60s Cultural Phenomenon*, Mitchell Beazley, London, 2003.

Forest Jean-Claude, *Barbarella*, Eric Losfeld Editions le Terrain Vague, Paris, 1964.

Garner Philippe, Mellor David Alan, *Antonioni's Blow Up*, Steidl, Gottingen, 2011.

Glaser Milton, *Graphic Design*, The Overlook Press, Woodstock New York, 1973.

Griffin Rick, McCelland Gordon, *Rick Griffin*, Paper Tiger an imprint of Dragon's World Ltd, Limpsfield, 1980.

Gorman Paul, *The Look: Adventures in Rock and Pop Fashion*, Adelita, London, 2006.

Gorman Paul, *Reasons to be Cheerful: the Life and Work of Barney Bubbles*, Adelita, London, 2008.

Gorman Paul, *Mr Freedom: Tommy Roberts, British Design Hero*, Adelita, London, 2012.

Grushkin Paul D, *The Art of Rock: Posters from Presley to Punk*, Artabras a division of Abbeville Press, New York ,London and Paris, 1987.

Harris Jennifer, Hyde Sarah, Smith Greg, *1966 and All That: Design and the Consumer in Britain, 1960-1969*, Trefoil Design library, London, 1986.

Harrod Tanya, Goldberg Roselee, *Carol McNicoll*, Lund Humphries, London 2003.

Harrod Tanya, *The Crafts in Britain in the Twentieth Century*, Yale University Press, New Haven & London, 1999.

Hieronimus Bob, *Inside the Yellow Submarine: the Making of the Beatles Animated Classic*, Krause Publications, Iola, 2002.

Hulanicki Barbara , *From A to Biba: The Autobiography of Barbara Hulanicki*, Hutchinson & Co, London, 1983.

Jones Barbara, *The Unsophisticated Arts*, Architectural Press, London, 1951.

Lambert Margaret, Marx Enid, *English Popular Art*, Batsford, London, 1951.

Lester Richard, *Boutique London, A History: King's Road to Carnaby Street*, ACC Editions, Woodbridge, 2010.

Lippard Lucy R, *Pop Art*, Thames and Hudson, London, 1966.

Livingston Marco, *Pop Art: A Continuing History*, Thames & Hudson, London, 1990.

Lobenthal Joel, *Radical Rags: Fashion of the Sixties*, Abbeville Press, New York, 1990.

Marechal Paul, Ed. *Andy Warhol – The Record Covers 1949 – 1987*, Catalogue Raisonne, Museum of Fine Arts , Montreal, Prestel USA, 2008.

Massey Anne, *The Independent Group: Modernism and Mass Culture in Britain, 1945-59*, Manchester University Press, 1995.

Melly George, *Revolt into Style*, Penguin Books, London, 1970.

Mellor David, *The Sixties Art Scene in London*, Phaidon Press in association with the Barbican Art Gallery, London, 1993.

Mulholland Neil, *The Cultural Devolution: Art in Britain in the Late Twentieth Century*, Ashgate, 2003.

Neville Richard, *Playpower*, Jonathan Cape, London, 1970.

Neville Richard, *Hippie Hippie Shake: the Dreams, the Trips, the Trials, the Love-ins, the Screw Ups: the Sixties*, W Heinemann, London, 1995.

Nuttall Jeff, *Bomb Culture*, Paladin, London, 1970.

Peake Tony, *Derek Jarman: A Biography*, Overlook Press, London, 1999.

Peellaert Guy, Thomas Pascal, *Pravda La Survireuse*, Eric Losfeld editions le Terrain Vague, Paris, 1968.

Powell Aubery, Thorgerson Storm, Mason Nick, *For the Love of Vinyl; the Art of Hipgnosis*, PictureBox Inc, Brooklyn NY, 2007.

Quant Mary, *Quant by Quant*, Cassell, London, 1966.

Quant Mary, *Mary Quant: My Autobiography*, Headline, 2012.

Hamilton Richard, *Collected Words*, Thames and Hudson, London, 1983.

Reed Jeremy, *The King of Carnaby Street: A Life of John Stevens*, Haus, London, 2010.

Rhodes Zandra, Knight Anne, *The Art of Zandra Rhodes*, Jonathan Cape, London, 1984.

Robb John, Craske Oliver, *Punk Rock: an Oral History*, Ebury Press, London, 2006.

Ross Aquilina Geoffrey, *The Day of the Peacock: Style for Men 1963-1973*, V&A Publications, London, 2011.

Rudd Natalie, *Peter Blake*, Tate Publishing, London, 2003.

Safer Samantha Erin, *Zandra Rhodes Textile Revolution: Medals, Wriggles and Pop 1961-1971*, Antique Collectors Club, Woodbridge, 2010.

Salter Tom, *Carnaby Street*, Margaret and Jack Hobbs, Walton-on-Thames, 1970.

Sandbrook Dominic, *Never had It So Good: A History of Britain From Suez to The Beatles*, Abacus, London, 2006.

Sandbrook Dominic, *White Heat: A History Of Britain In The Swinging Sixties*, Abacus, London, 2007.

Savage Jon, Reid Jamie, *Up They Rise: the Incomplete Works of Jamie Reid*, Faber and Faber, London, 1987.

Stern Jane and Michael, *Sixties People*, Alfred A Knopf, New York, 1990.

Thorgerson Storm, Dean Roger, The Album Cover Album, Dragon's World, Limpsfield, 1977.

Thorgerson Storm, *The Work of Hipgnosis: Walk Away Rene*, Paper Tiger, Dragon's World ltd Imprint, Limpsfield, 1978.

Twiggy, *Twiggy: An Autobiography*, Paperback edition, Mayflower Books, London, 1976.

Whiteley Nigel, *Pop Design: Modernism to Mod*, Design Council, London 1987.

York Peter, *Style Wars*, Sidgwick and Jackson, London, 1980.

ACKNOWLEDGEMENTS

We especially wish to thank the photographer for the book, Jonathan Richards of Foto Theme, London, for his good natured tolerance, patience and painstaking work, James Smith of ACC Editions for commissioning the book, and our patient and long-suffering editor Catherine Britton. Also a big thank you to the staff of the Fashion and Textile Museum, Bermondsey, London, for their enthusiastic support and advice, particularly Dennis Nothdruft, Alison McCann and Celia Joicey, and the book's excellent designers Orna Frommer-Dawson and Geoff Windram of John and Orna Designs, London.

Numerous others have been extremely generous with their contributions of time, knowledge and images and in particular we would like to thank: Simon and Mel Andrews, David Bailey, Angela Brill, H. Kirk Brown and Jill Wiltse, Trevor and Elaine Chamberlain, Michael Eftihiou, Duggie Fields, Philippe Garner, David Kewn and Jonathan Knight of Gordon Maxwell Restoration and Conservation, Andrew Logan, David Morris, Catherine Moriarty, Pamla Motown, Mick Milligan, Cliff Richards, Zandra Rhodes, Shanna Shelby, Keith Wainwright.

Geoff Rayner in 1962

Aged fifteen as the first reverberations of the Youthquake began in 1956, Geoff Rayner grew up in the Rock 'n' Roll and Pop years of the late 1950s and 1960s. He spent his youth in west London, where he was an habitué Of the Eel Pie Island Club, Twickenham, and the Crawdaddy at the Station Hotel, Richmond, where bands like the Rolling Stones played regularly. The Island Club and the Richmond coffee bar scene were magnets for students from the local art schools, amongst them Pete Townshend, Eric Clapton and Rod Stewart, and at that time Geoff met many later well-known sixties people, like the graphic designer Barney Bubbles (Colin Fulcher) Ian MacLagan of the Small Faces (Little Mac), the DJ Annie Nightingale and members of the Manfred Mann group.

The Eel Pie Island Club's proprietor Arthur Chisnall became a lifelong friend, and through him, in 1964, Geoff became involved in one of the first sixties' community theatre projects, based in the Paddington area of London, where he met and worked with the writer and broadcaster Jill Neville, sister of the founder of *Oz* magazine, Richard Neville.

In 1967 he was introduced to the American Ed Berman, later founder of Inter-Action, with whom he continued to develop community theatre work. That Christmas, instead of the usual nativity play, he and Ed jointly produced and directed for Independent Television, a children's 'alternative' Christmas show, Super Santa.

In the later sixties he became increasingly involved with London's counter-culture, and in 1972, with help from Arthur Chisnall and workers from the 'alternative' information centre 'BIT', he successfully squatted a large semi-derelict house in the Elephant and Castle area of London where he set up a well-respected Free School and children's theatre project, which developed links with the anti-psychiatrist R. D. Lang's Philadelphia Association, and whose manifesto and PR material was designed by the well-known anarchist illustrator Cliff Harper. Considering the many pressures of the times, the project survived well into the early 1980s.

Geoff has always subsidised his various projects by selling art and antiques, and in the late 1980s he began to deal and collect design from the post-war era, setting up the Target Gallery in 1994 with Richard Chamberlain, an expert in post-war culture, specialising in textile design. Their gallery broke new ground with a number of well-received pioneering exhibitions, notably, in 1999, 'Design in Tandem: The Work of Robin and Lucienne Day', and in 2001, 'Reconstruction: Designers in Britain 1945-1951'.

Geoff and Richard also jointly curated and co-authored, with Annamarie Stapleton, the exhibitions and accompanying books, 'Austerity to Affluence: British Art and Design 1945-1962', and 'Artists' Textiles in Britain 1945-1970', both held at the Fine Art Society, London, in 1997 and 2003 respectively. Again with Annamarie, they curated an exhibition held at the Fine Art Society in 2006 of the work of the artist, textile designer and manufacturer Alastair Morton. Since then Geoff and Richard have been consultants for the documentary film on the work of the designers Robin and Lucienne Day, 'Contemporary Days', and the memorial exhibition of their work, 'Robin and Lucienne Day: Design and the Modern Interior', held in 2011 at Pallant House Art Gallery, Chichester, and the PM Gallery, Ealing, London.

In 2009, Geoff, Richard and Annamarie co-authored a book on the work of the textile designer Jacqueline Groag, and in 2012, a revised and expanded edition of *Artists' Textiles: 1945-1976*, a survey of textile design by artists in the post-war years. Geoff, Richard and Annamarie's most recent project has been the 2012 exhibition of Pop design at the Fashion and Textile Museum, Bermondsey, London.

Annamarie is a specialist in nineteenth- and twentieth-century design and contemporary crafts. A director of the Fine Art Society, she is the author of John Moyr Smith: A Victorian Designer, and is editor of the Decorative Arts Society Journal. A member of the Great Britain rowing team at the 1996 Atlanta Olympic Games, she is now Deputy Chairman of British Rowing and a trustee of the British Paralympic Association.